Praise for THE CONFIDENCE FACTOR

"Tom Mullins greatly impressed me when I met him in person, and I pray that his devotional book will be a blessing to you."

—DR. BILLY GRAHAM
Billy Graham Evangelistic Association, Best-Selling Author of
The Journey: How to Live by Faith in an Uncertain World

"Helping people feel more confident is a tremendous gift that few leaders pass on to others. Tom Mullins has that ability. Every day I watch him uplift people. Now it's your turn. Read this book and give your confidence a boost."

—DR. JOHN C. MAXWELL
Best-Selling Author, Speaker, Founder of
INJOY Stewardship Services and EQUIP

"Tom Mullins exudes bold faith and a winning confidence in God. So it is not surprising that the book you hold in your hands pulsates with life and power. *The Confidence Factor* will challenge, encourage, and inspire you on a daily basis to live in spiritual victory."

—DR. JACK GRAHAM
Pastor of Prestonwood Baptist Church, Plano, Texas

"Tom Mullins has cracked the code for all of us who desire never again to give in to the fear of the moment. *The Confidence Factor* is a must-read for those of us who dare to step into the future with resilience and intensive trust."

—DR. JAY STRACK
Founder and President of Student Leadership University
(www.studentleadership.net)

"Tom Mullins is gifted by God to inspire not only self-confidence, but God-confidence. He reminds us that what may seem like an unreachable star is, in fact, a possibility because a guiding light is available to all who will believe for the best."

—JAMES ROBISON
Founder and President of LIFE Outreach International,
Fort Worth, Texas

"Tom Mullins is one of the best leaders I know. His new book, *The Confidence Factor: The Key to Developing the Winning Edge in Life*, is a classic. No one exudes practical biblical God-centered confidence more than Dr. Mullins. He is the right man to write this book."

—DR. JERRY FALWELL
President/Chancellor of Liberty University, Lynchburg, Virginia

"Few men in our generation have earned the right to speak to us about confidence. Tom Mullins is one of these men. His life and the arenas in which he enters serve as proof that he has been raised up to speak to all of us. I believe in Tom Mullins and in this exciting, compelling book."

—DR. RONNIE W. FLOYD
Senior Pastor of First Baptist Church of Springdale and
The Church at Pinnacle Hills, Arkansas

"*The Confidence Factor* will empower you to combine belief and balance, truth and tactics for effective Christian living. Dr. Tom Mullins teaches the Christian leader how to build self-confidence, even in the midst of life's toughest challenges. A must-read for those who plan to win in the game of life."

—DR. JAMES O. DAVIS
Cofounder/President/CEO of Global Pastors Network

"Tom Mullins was a successful football coach who understood the importance of 'confidence' when it came to winning games. He also understands the 'confidence factor' in serving the Lord and building a great church. Tom has rock-solid confidence because he has committed himself to the Lord Jesus Christ, so he has confidence that God will bless and use him. This is a wonderful book that communicates to every pastor and church leader the necessity of building confidence to build a winning team in Christian service."

—DR. ELMER TOWNS
Vice President and Dean of the School of Religion,
Liberty University, Lynchburg, Virginia

"Tom Mullins is a leader! Over the past few years I have had the opportunity to spend time with Tom and have seen the 'confidence factor' at work in his life. He works and plays with confidence, and knows what he is talking about when it comes to being a consistent productive leader. In his book, *The Confidence Factor*, Tom lets us take a peek at what has made him an incredible coach and mentor to so many people. He opens the reader's eyes to the hope for enduring hardship and reveals the true foundation that we can build our lives around. Tom is a practitioner of confident leadership. I will re-read this one for years to come."

—BILLY HORNSBY
Director of Association of Related Churches

THE CONFIDENCE FACTOR

The Key to Developing the Winning Edge in Life

TOM MULLINS

NELSON BOOKS
A Division of Thomas Nelson Publishers
Since 1798

www.thomasnelson.com

Published in Nashville, Tennessee, by Thomas Nelson, Inc.

Nelson Books titles may be purchased in bulk for educational, business, fund-raising or sales promotional use. For information, please e-mail SpecialMarkets@ThomasNelson.com.

All Scripture quotations, unless otherwise indicated, are taken from the Holy Bible, New International Version®. NIV®. Copyright © 1973, 1978, 1984 by International Bible Society. Used by permission of Zondervan. All rights reserved.

Scripture quotations marked NKJV are taken from the New King James Version®. Copyright © 1982 by Thomas Nelson, Inc. Used by permission. All rights reserved.

The Scripture quotation marked NASB has been taken from the New American Standard Bible®, Copyright © 1960, 1962, 1963, 1968, 1971, 1972, 1973, 1975, 1977, 1995 by The Lockman Foundation (www.Lockman.org). Used by permission.

The Scripture quotation marked AMPLIFIED is taken from the Amplified® Bible, Copyright © 1954, 1958, 1962, 1964, 1965, 1987 by The Lockman Foundation (www.Lockman.org). Used by permission.

The Scripture quotation marked THE MESSAGE is taken from The Message by Eugene H. Peterson, (copyright 1993, 1994, 1995, 1996, 2000, 2001, 2002) and is used by permission of NavPress Publishing Group.

The Scripture quotation marked KJV is from The Holy Bible, King James Version.

Scripture passages marked COACH are the author's paraphrase.

Library of Congress Cataloging-in-Publication Data

Mullins, Tom.
   The confidence factor : the key to developing the winning edge in life / Tom Mullins.
      p. cm.
ISBN-13: 978-0-7852-1859-3 (hardcover)
ISBN-10: 0-7852-1859-9
   1. Confidence—Religious aspects—Christianity. I. Title.
BV4647.C63M85 2006
248.4--dc22
2006030531

Printed in the United States of America
07 08 09 10 **QWM** 5 4 3 2

I dedicate this book to my wife, Donna.

*I consider myself so blessed to have such
a great woman of faith by my side.*

*For the last forty-one years, she has
consistently inspired me with her faith and
confidence in Christ Jesus. Her belief in me
has always reinforced my confidence to face
the challenge of life with the winning edge.*

Contents

Acknowledgments

FIRST AND FOREMOST, I THANK JESUS CHRIST FOR HIS LIFE, love, and sacrifice that have given me confidence to follow Him and find my destiny.

My family's support has inspired me greatly. Thank you to my son Todd, my daughter Noelle, my daughter-in-law Julie, and my grandson Jefferson. Their love for me, and their unity in service to our King is a reward I will carry to eternity . . . I am so blessed.

I also want to thank Carolyn Master, my assistant, who helped me so much. From draft to draft, this project was truly a labor of love and commitment.

Thanks also to Dr. Dan Light and Brent Cole for their endless hours of input and guidance and for their confidence to see this project through to completion.

Thanks to Victor Oliver and his team at Thomas Nelson for working so diligently and with excellence to get this book done well.

I want to express gratitude to my church family, Christ Fellowship. Without their faithfulness and love over the years, I would not have the confidence to lead our church to impact our world with the love and message of Jesus Christ.

Finally, thanks to my mother for her great faith that set the course of my life. She has always encouraged me to discover the true confidence factor found in a life lived under the power and authority of Jesus Christ.

CONFIDENCE PRODUCES THE WINNING EDGE

CHAPTER ONE

Living in the Zone

I WAS SITTING AT A BASKETBALL GAME IN LEXINGTON, Kentucky, but I wasn't there to watch the Wildcats. It was "Pistol Pete" Maravich, one of the greatest college basketball players of all time, who drew me to the coliseum that day. He scored more points than any college player in history. Even before the three-point line became part of the game, Pete Maravich averaged forty-four points a game.

Earlier that day it was reported that he was injured, and as I awaited the start of the game, I wondered if he would play up to his caliber. During warm-ups, I noticed he had a bad limp, but when the whistle blew, Pistol Pete started lighting up the scoreboard in legendary style.

Kentucky double-teamed him all night, but they couldn't keep him from scoring. I grinned at a friend sitting beside me. "Pete is 'in the zone,'" I said. By night's end, he had scored forty-four points. His injury had no hold on him, nor did the opposition. He was unstoppable.

When a player like Pete Maravich is in the zone, he believes he will succeed. As a result, he usually does. Sports greats are notorious for this.

Michael Jordan lived in the zone, especially during championship games. He won six NBA Championships with the Chicago Bulls because of his uncanny ability to sink the make-or-break shots with seconds left on the clock. When the game was on the line, no one wanted the ball more. He believed he would come through.

With seventy-one holes behind him and the world before him, Jack Nicklaus sunk his putt on the eighteenth green at Augusta for a record-winning eighteenth professional major tournament. No golfer played in the zone more than Jack. He is the only one to win each of the four Grand Slam tournaments at least three times.

His ability to make the perfect shot or sink the decisive putt earned him an amazing seventy-three PGA tour victories and a combined twenty-six professional major championship titles (between the regular and senior tours) before his 2005 retirement. Yet I know Jack is an extremely focused man in other areas of life—and I know this springs from confidence.

I remember challenging Jack to a free throw contest one after-noon following a high-school football practice where I coached his sons. He agreed and we made our way to the gymnasium. I grabbed the ball and jogged over to the free throw line where I made eight of my ten shots—pretty good for an old football player.

Then Jack stood up and took the ball. Intently he fixed his eyes on that rim then lowered his gaze to the ball. He took a few bounces then tossed his first shot. He made it . . . and then proceeded to make the other nine in the same fashion.

After seeing him sink ten consecutive free throws, I encouraged him to keep going as long as he could. Meanwhile, I tried everything I could to distract his shot—clapping, yelling, stomping my feet. It didn't matter; he was in the zone—so much so that he sank thirty in a row before finally missing.

I mention these athletes because a common factor lies at the core of their great accomplishments: confidence. Without question it is the difference maker in any sporting event, from basketball to golf to the Olympic Games. It sets the great athletes apart from the rest.

Incidentally, confidence is equally vital in everyday life. It can set you apart and make the difference between a good and bad decision or between having an optimistic or pessimistic attitude. Ultimately, it determines whether tough times make or break us.

Filled with confidence, we find courage to face challenges and to overcome them. We see clearly to do what is necessary. That's because confidence enhances our perspective. With it we see the upside of our circumstances. We see potential in others, and we see it in ourselves. We see the ultimate impact of our actions. These encourage us to move forward despite our fears or shortcomings. Confidence gives us stamina; it boosts our endurance. It reminds us we can keep on hanging, even if only by a thread.

Finally, confidence helps us perform at our highest level. With it we remain focused on what is most important.

The Foundation of Confidence

I was struck by the words of Edward Teller, the famous nuclear scientist, who said, "When you come to the end of all the light you know, and it's time to step into the darkness of the unknown, faith is knowing that one of two things shall happen: Either you will be given something solid to stand on, or you will be taught to fly."[1]

Life is full of both darkness and light. Circumstances can lead us into green pastures, and they can lead us through unknown valleys where shadows are far more prominent than sunlight. In either case, confidence is necessary in order to have the attitude we need to take action—and often that crucial confidence must be found in something greater than ourselves. That's why faith is so important.

There's no doubt that great athletes—the Pete Maraviches and Michael Jordans and Jack Nicklauses—are confident in their athletic abilities. They should be. Their abilities enable them to succeed most of the time. In the same way, there's no doubt some of us are better equipped than others for dealing with life's ups and downs. These are admirable qualities we're talking about, and there is no downplaying the value that exists in acquiring them. But no matter how self-confident we are, no matter how positive or strong-willed we stay, our armor still has chinks. The sudden death of a loved one. The discovery of a lump. The loss of a job. A false accusation. Whatever it is, when it hits us, our confidence can quickly fade.

Sometimes it seems impossible to find confidence when we're staring at an X-ray of a malignant tumor or weeping over the grave of someone we just lost. Sometimes strength and hope seem so far away and the day's reality seems so close. In such times we would all like to summon another source of strength. We want a foundation to stand on that is more stable than our own resources can provide. By faith, we have one.

Our Source of Confidence

The goal of this book is not to help you discover where you *lack* confidence. I think most of us already know that. This book, however, will help you to rediscover some of the truths that can be forgotten when life's pain and pressures mount. The goal of the book is to remind you of the true foundation of your confidence—in yourself, in relationships, in crisis, in tomorrow. With this firm foundation, it is possible to stand strong, no matter how fierce the wind.

Even the most confident individuals can lose sight of the truth. The psalms are filled with honest cries for help from a king who at times preferred to die rather than face his troubles. David confessed time and again that he couldn't stand—that he didn't want to stand—without God's strength.

The great prophet Elijah, who called down fire from heaven and executed 450 false prophets, asked God to take his life just two days later. He was overcome with fear and fatigue. God replied, "The journey *is* too great for you" (1 Kings 19:7 NKJV), and then He provided Elijah with new strength and direction. The prophet's confidence was restored (1 Kings 18–19).

When the journey seems too much to bear, we have a choice. We can rely on our wits to see us through, or we can summon something far steadier. Our bodies and our wills can withstand a lot. We are fearfully and wonderfully made. But God never intended that we take this journey alone. Nor is it His purpose for us to crawl from trial to trial our entire lives. He gave us Jesus so that we can stand and walk through each day in confidence no matter what comes our way.

Can we actually live in the zone? The apostle Paul, who maintained a great attitude and displayed confidence almost beyond belief, lived there. He understood the true source of his contentment, peace, and strength. To the people of the church at Philippi he declared, "I can do all things through Christ who strengthens me" (Phil. 4:13 NKJV).

Paul's source of confidence, no matter what he faced, was Jesus. Jesus assures us, "I came to give you life and to give you the winning edge" (John 10:10 COACH). I want to live with that winning edge. And I want you to live with it as well.

The goal of *The Confidence Factor* is to help you to discover the confidence that Paul discovered and to help you understand that Christ came to give you the winning edge in life. Then you, too, will discover and fulfill your destiny and impact the world for Christ.

I designed this book with short chapters so it could be used as a personal devotion or a group teaching tool. If you take each new principle in small doses, carefully considering how it applies to your life, before long you will see a tangible change in your attitude, your self-confidence, and your faith in God.

My hope is that as you read this book, each chapter adds more confidence and greater purpose to your journey. As we observe people who lived out their faith despite hard and sometimes impossible circumstances, my prayer is that you would aspire to follow their example in your own life. At the end of our time together, may the true Source of confidence, Jesus Christ, become more accessible to you every day until God's ultimate purpose for your life is fulfilled.

> I can do all things through
> Christ who strengthens me.
>
> —PHILIPPIANS 4:13 (NKJV)

CHAPTER TWO

Your Journey Matters

ALL OF US ARE ON A JOURNEY OF FAITH. IN HIS WORD, GOD expresses His desire that we travel on the right path, the one path that leads to Him. How can we be confident we are on the right path? There are many who say the path doesn't matter just as long as you're sincere. Ultimately, they say, all paths will get you to the same place. When people say this, I think of the following story.

In 1846, a group of eighty-seven emigrants started on a 2500-mile journey from Springfield, Illinois to California. They carried with them a guidebook, *The Emigrants' Guide to Oregon and California* by Lansford Hastings, which proposed a trail they believed would save them weeks of travel time.

The party crossed the prairies along the Blue River and then headed north toward the plains of the Platte River. When they reached the Platte, they headed westward. On the north bank of the Platte, they encountered a man named James Clyman. Under Hastings' instructions, he was heading east from California, meeting traveling parties headed west with a letter of warning: the Hastings route was not suitable, and they should take another route.

Ignoring Clyman's advice, the Donner Party pressed on through Wyoming and toward the Sierra Nevada Mountains. When they arrived at what they thought was a suitable pass over the majestic range, they realized it would be too difficult for those traveling by wagon to get through. They pressed on anyway . . . until a blizzard hit and trapped them in over twenty feet of snow. Of the original group, forty-one of them died. Those who did make it survived by eating the flesh of the deceased.

In a letter to her friend back east, survivor Virginia Reed concluded with an understated salutation: "Remember, never take no cutoffs and hurry along as fast as you can."[1]

We live in a world where there are many proposed paths of faith. While each of us longs to know and experience Truth, the world promotes a notion that there are many alternatives to finding it. It can be confusing knowing what path to take, as Thomas expressed in the Gospel of John. "Lord," he said to Jesus, "we don't know where you are going, so how can we know the way?" (John 14:5).

Jesus replied, "I am the way and the truth and the life. No one comes to the Father except through Me" (vs. 6). In essence, He was saying, "Many claim to know the way to fulfillment, but I am the only way for you to discover the purpose that God has for you. Put your confidence in Me."

Then He says, "I am the truth." The word "truth" means a complete, absolute center or focus of real knowledge. Nothing comes before it. Nothing will come after it or can be added to it. It is complete in itself. Jesus was saying, "I am the absolute revelation of this truth you seek. I am the one who can give you a life that will satisfy the deepest longings of your soul and help you embrace your destiny."

Claims of Truth

We live in a society with various conflicting religions and philosophies, all staking a claim on the truth. Yet the Scriptures warn us of these various ideologies: "There is a way that seems right to a man, but in the end it leads to death" (Prov. 14:12).

In John chapter five, Jesus visits the Pool of Bethesda in Jerusalem. This was a regular place of gathering for people who were hoping to be healed of some kind of affliction. According to legend, an angel came to the pool and stirred the water from time to time, and the first person to enter the troubled waters would receive instantaneous healing.

At the pool, Jesus struck up a conversation with one crippled man, who explained that he had no one to help him into the water. Then Jesus told him to get up and walk. It was this encounter with Christ that made the difference in his life.

There are two factors that distinguish Jesus from all the other world religions and philosophies:

1. ALL OTHER PHILOSOPHIES AND WORLD RELIGIONS FOCUS ON WHAT WE DO

If we are good, they say, we will receive goodness in return, now and in the afterlife. For the Christian, goodness is about what God has already done for us through Jesus Christ. He has provided salvation for us—His perfect goodness became ours. Thus, our only response need be that of embracing the gift and following Him with faith.

We can do nothing to earn God's grace. We can't purify ourselves or improve our standing with God by a lifetime of good deeds. It's only through Jesus Christ who died on the cross that we can find richness of life now and forever (Eph. 2:8–9).

My wife, Donna, came to know a woman who had grown up as a Buddhist. Jill began to attend a Bible class in our church to "learn about Jesus." She had a sincere desire to understand Christianity and she faithfully pursued her search. Even though Jill had been raised under the principles of another religion, she had a heart and mind that was honest and hungry for the truth.

From time to time, Donna would talk with Jill and ask, "Are you ready to give your heart to Christ?"

"Not yet," Jill would reply.

The women at the study continued to love and pray for Jill, and one day she came up to Donna and announced, "I did it!" After two agonizing years of searching and asking God to make Himself known to her, Jill made the life-changing decision to become a follower of Jesus Christ. Today, she is an active member of our church and is fulfilling her destiny.

2. JESUS IS THE ONLY GUIDE WE CAN TRUST

Lansford Hastings, who published the guidebook used by the Donner Party, did not make the journey himself prior to the book's publication, which made him a tragically unreliable "expert." After writing the guidebook, however, Hastings traveled most of his route by horseback with a few companions and determined there was no way people in wagons could travel the route.

Realizing his horrible mistake, Hastings put up signs that said, "Warning! Do Not Come This Way." He also sent riders on horseback, carrying a letter inviting them to take a different course. However, history tells us the Donner Party stubbornly pressed on, ignoring all the warnings. Their poor judgment led to death.[2]

We also have to be careful not to ignore the signs before us. For "holy men of God spoke as they were moved by the Holy Spirit" (2 Peter 1:21 NKJV). Through His prophets, God has given us guidance, principles, precepts, and warning signs to direct our lives, and in God's time, these teachings have been gathered together to form the Bible. Today, we live in a world inhabited by skeptics who say, "Why rely on that old road map? Today you can write your own."

When people bring up ideas like this, I like to tell them about a Yale law school graduate by the name of Lee Strobel. This professing atheist became upset when his wife began attending church, and he decided to join her in order to point out the flaws and inconsistencies in the church's teachings. Lee dug into the Bible study materials, bent on proving his wife simpleminded.

Then something began to happen that he didn't expect. All the exposure to God's Word began changing his heart. He couldn't resist the effect it was having on him. Eventually, he was radically transformed, and he became a believer in the Lord Jesus Christ.[3] In response to this amazing transformation, he wrote *The Case for Christ*, one of the most profound books of apologetics in defense of the Christian faith.

The truth of God's Word has been time-tested and proven. It continues to be so today. Archaeological digs regularly turn up evidence that verifies the prophecies found only within the Bible. Every time scholars dig deep, with honesty of heart, they come to see the validity of the Word of God. In the very least, they cannot scientifically refute it. So often we search tirelessly for something that is so simple to see, if only we took the time to look.

We should be cautious about taking shortcuts on our journey of faith. There is only one sure path. And when the signs are confusing, three simple principles give us confidence to continue on our faith journey, even when it seems like the long way:

1. Follow the right guide: Jesus.
2. Follow the right guidebook: the Bible.
3. Travel with the right companions: other firm believers in the faith.

If you have never committed your life to the guidance of Jesus Christ, you now have an opportunity to begin walking with Him on your journey. I invite you to resolve it right now in prayer:

Lord, please forgive me of my sins, for trying to take my own path and missing the mark You have for me. I now accept Your invitation to begin my journey of confidence in You as my Lord and Savior. I trust You to give me the wisdom and guidance to face all of the questions and conflicts that may come my way, believing that You will be faithful to provide all I need. In the name of our Lord, Jesus Christ, Amen.

You have made known to me the
path of life; you will fill me with joy
in your presence, with eternal
pleasures at your right hand.

—PSALM 16:11

CHAPTER THREE
Huddle Up with God

I RAN ONTO THE FIELD AS THE TEAM WAS BREAKING FROM the huddle. I didn't know what play had been called. I didn't know the formation, and I didn't know the snap count. The quarterback yelled at me and pointed where I was supposed to line up. Then the ball was snapped, and the quarterback turned to hand me the ball. I didn't know where to run, and I was quickly tackled for a loss. That day I learned the importance of getting into the huddle. Otherwise, I would never know where to be when the ball is snapped or where to run when handed the ball.

Miss the huddle, and you will waver and even get knocked down where you stand.

This principle works the same in life. To gain the confidence we need to meet life's responsibilities head-on, we need to "huddle up" with God every day. In the sixth chapter of the Gospel of Matthew, Jesus teaches us how to do this, and He shows us five benefits.

BENEFIT #1: A BETTER PERSPECTIVE

"Our Father which art in heaven," Jesus begins His prayer, "hallowed be Thy name" (Matt. 6:9 KJV). By acknowledging His Father in heaven, Jesus acknowledged that His Father was *above* all else in His life and that He is both omniscient and omnipotent. By recognizing

His Father's name as holy, He was acknowledging that God the Father was Jesus' foremost priority.

When we begin our days by recognizing God's place in the universe and in our lives, we gain a better perspective about everything else that comes our way. We can see that life is not about our individual circumstances; it's about what God wants to do *in* us and *through* those circumstances. This helps us gain a better perspective: how our lives fit into God's "Master plan." By focusing on who God is and what He is capable of doing on our behalf, opportunities come into view that inspire the confidence we need to follow His lead.

In football, it isn't possible for each player to see everything happening on the field. Things often happen so fast that you can only react and hope your reactions are right. When I was coaching, I quickly realized the sidelines were not the best place to observe the game. The best view is from high in the press box. There, you can look down and see the whole field and all the players' activities.

The same could be said of God. He sees our circumstances in ways we can't. He knows our strengths and weaknesses better than we do. And because of that, He knows exactly where we should be in every situation. He knows where we need to "line up" and the perfect timing for each activity in our lives so that His game plan is carried out. Our responsibility is to trust His perspective. While there will be moments where we seem to see something differently than He does, the more we get to know God's character, the more confident we will be in trusting Him.

BENEFIT #2: A GREATER PURPOSE

"Thy Kingdom come, Thy will be done on earth as it is in heaven" (Matt. 6:10 KJV). By getting in the huddle with God each day, He reminds us that we are being called to a higher purpose—something more than just a good career and a healthy body and a loving family. While these things are important to Him, God is working on something bigger than the scope of our individual well-being, and He invites us to be a part of it.

If you've ever played a team sport, you know that personal accolades aren't as important as a team victory. As the Great Coach of the Universe, God is most interested in team victory.

One of the things I loved most about playing and coaching football was striving for victory as part of a team. Personal accomplishments were important, and as a coach, I made sure we celebrated the major ones along the way (just as God does with us). However, the real celebrations took place when we won the games. I think God is like that too. While He desires the very best for us as individuals, ultimately, He desires us to give our lives over to the greater purpose of furthering His Kingdom.

Jesus urges us, "Therefore do not worry, saying, 'What shall we eat?' or 'What shall we drink?' or 'What shall we wear?' . . . For your heavenly Father knows that you need all these things. But seek first the kingdom of God, and all these things shall be added to you" (Matt. 6:31–33 NKJV).

Seeking God's Kingdom first means that at times circumstances won't turn out as we had hoped they would. Yet, the more we offer ourselves to God's greater purpose, the more we see His hand at work, and consequently the more confident we will become in His plans for us and for the world.

BENEFIT #3: DAILY STRENGTH

"Give us this day our daily bread" (Matt. 6:11 NKJV). Huddling up with God each day gives us not only perspective and purpose; it gives us strength. God knows what we need when we need it, and He is there to provide for us. Sometimes He gives us strength enough only for that day to teach us to depend upon Him daily. "Trust me today,"

He is saying to us. "Don't lean on your understanding of your circumstances. Have confidence that I am Almighty God, and I *will* direct your path today" (Prov. 3:5–6 COACH).

In human terms, this might seem a bit manipulative of God. It can feel unnatural to be dependent on someone and something we cannot touch or see. At first it seems to breed more doubt and anxiety than confidence.

King David found it difficult to rely on God when the walls seemed to be caving in. He admitted to God that he was troubled and anxious and that he feared for his life. But each time he also acknowledged that God came through, and that we can be confident in His help and provision.

When God delivered David from Abimelech, who wanted to kill him, David declared, "This poor man cried out, and the LORD heard him, and saved him out of all his troubles. Oh, taste and see that the LORD is good; blessed is the man who trusts in Him!" (Ps. 34:6, 8 NKJV)

Why is it that when we have a need, we run everywhere else before running to God? Is it because our strength, our confidence, is found elsewhere? Only we can answer for ourselves, but when God is the first place we turn, He is faithful to come through in ways that display His goodness. "I would have lost heart," wrote David, "unless I had believed that I would see the goodness of the LORD in the land of the living. Wait on the LORD; be of good courage, and He shall strengthen your heart; wait, I say, on the LORD!" (Ps. 27:13–14 NKJV)

BENEFIT #4: A FRESH START

"And forgive us our debts, as we forgive our debtors" (Matt. 6:12 KJV). Every time we get in the huddle with God, we can be confident He will give us a fresh start.

I played high-school football in southern Ohio, where they take football pretty seriously. I started at defense my freshman year as a monsterback—what you might call a "strong safety" today. I was also the backup punter.

We were playing one of the toughest Cincinnati schools when our punter got hurt. I had never punted in a game, but when it came time I stood back, ready to receive the snap. I thought, *I'm going to set an all-time punting record for my high school. They've never seen a ball go as far as this ball is going to go.*

Then came the snap. I caught it, dropped the ball softly into position, kicked as hard as I could . . . and missed the ball. Not only that, but I fell on my back and knocked the wind out of myself. The ball went rolling between the guard's feet, and the opponents recovered the fumble.

Now, my coach was huge. Coach Young was about 285 pounds and six feet, four inches tall. He used to wear those old-fashioned high-top cleats. The last thing I wanted to do was to face him on the sidelines. Fortunately, I started on defense, so I got to stay on the field. I'll never forget going into the next huddle, feeling so embarrassed as I stood there, trying to get my breath back. Then one of the captains said, "That's okay, Mullins. We're gonna make up for it. Go out there now and knock somebody's head off!" My teammates gave me another chance, and I didn't have to face the coach right away.

When we huddle up with our Heavenly Father, it doesn't matter how much we've messed up; He is there to forgive us and help us move on toward victory. He wants us to be confident that we can come to Him every day, no matter what we've done or how embarrassed we feel.

BENEFIT #5: COURAGE

"Lead us not into temptation but deliver us from evil" (Matt. 6:13 KJV). Here Jesus gives us the final benefit of huddling with

God. I find courage when I'm with God—no matter how tough the struggle, how great the demands, or how much my body wants to give up because He is on my side. God has promised us that when He is our teammate, we will be overcomers. "If God be for me," Paul says in Romans 8:31, "who can mess with me?" (COACH).

I loved hunting with my grandfather when I was young. We often hunted at night so that the dogs could chase raccoons. One time, we could hear that the dogs had treed a raccoon long off in the distance, and Grandpa asked me to stay put until he came back. Nervously I pleaded, "No, Grandpa. I want to go with you."

But he was unrelenting and told me to wait where I was until he returned. With my grandfather, I only needed to be told once. I stood there with my back to a tree, trying to be strong. As he walked into the dark and the light from his flashlight began to fade, fear began to twist my heart. I saw all kinds of shadows and images taunting me in the trees. I even picked up a stick to defend myself from the wild beasts around me.

Before long, the dogs stopped barking. I knew my grandfather would return soon. Off in the distance I saw a flicker of light bouncing along toward me, and as the light grew brighter, the courage in my heart got bigger. As long as Grandpa was with me, I had all the courage in the world. I found confidence from being in the presence of someone I knew loved and cared for me.

My grandfather was bigger than life but greater still is our Heavenly Father, who will stand with us no matter what forest we find ourselves in and give us courage to stand tall and face the shadows.

Life seems full of dark seasons when the light of God's voice is distant and fading. It takes courage in this time to remain confident that He will speak to us again. It also takes courage to remember that no matter how many shadows surround us, God has promised He will never abandon us. He is by our side in good times and in bad.

Life has a way of making us forget this fact. And this is why He asks us to huddle up with Him regularly: so that we will remember He is beside us, and so that we will know how to respond no matter what life looks like. When we huddle up with God, we have the confidence to execute the plays of life with excellence.

Come near to God and
He will come near to you.

—JAMES 4:8

CHAPTER FOUR

The Confidence of a Champion

THE SOUND OF A NATIONAL ANTHEM REVERBERATED IN the air as the crowd focused on the platform at the center of the Olympic stadium, where the medal winners stood. Head and shoulders above the rest was the champion, the recipient of the gold medal, whose lip trembled slightly as she mouthed "The Star Spangled Banner."

No, there is no other thrill quite like that of seeing one of your nation's own being lauded as the "best of the best."

How does an athlete get to be number one? Many factors are involved, of course, but one commonality that stands out: they have confidence. And I am convinced that this championship confidence is available to every Christian.

God's intention is to transform problems into possibilities and troubles into triumphs. That's what God did for the believers of the first-century church, and we applaud them still today. There is no reason why we in the twenty-first-century church cannot perform at the same level. Here are some of the main ways we can:

1. WE GAIN CONFIDENCE WHEN WE HAVE
THE RIGHT COACH

Jeremy Wariner won gold medals in the 400-meter dash and the 4x400 relay at the 2004 Olympics in Athens. Described by sports commentators as having run "a perfect race," Wariner really caught my attention in a recent interview when he said that he ran the race just the way his coach wanted him to. He recalled working the curve better than he had all year and finished with a good kick.

Wariner's coach, Clyde Hart, was the same guy who coached Michael Johnson, considered by most experts to be the greatest quarter miler of all time. Johnson won back-to-back gold medals in the 1996 and 2000 Olympics. Johnson also helped to train Wariner for the 2004 Olympic Games.

In the 400-meter race, Otis Harris, Wariner's teammate and his stiffest competition, got off to a great start and led the race into the final turn. But Wariner kept to the plan Coach Hart had taught him. He hung back and waited to kick it into gear down the stretch. When it came time, he passed Harris and pulled away for the win.

2. WE GAIN CONFIDENCE WHEN WE FOLLOW
THE RIGHT TRAINING PRINCIPLES

When asked what he said to Wariner before the final race, Michael Johnson said: "My advice is to continue doing exactly the things he's done to get to this point. Many young athletes get to the Olympics and feel they need to change something in order to be competitive. More often than not, these changes prove to be detrimental to the athlete's performance."[1] Wariner learned to trust that his training would prepare him for the race. When race time came, he ran with primed confidence.

3. WE GAIN CONFIDENCE WHEN WE HAVE
THE RIGHT ATTITUDE

"You've got to go in there with confidence," Wariner said to reporters at the Olympics. "Coach Hart has been able to teach that to me."[2]

In his own mind and heart, Wariner was already a winner. He didn't let his thinking drift to doubt and insecurity. He remained focused and determined. There was no "maybe."

When I followed the story of Wariner and a few of the other Olympic champions, I couldn't help but recognize the consistent way their coaching, training, and attitude related to living a Christian life of championship caliber. In fact, there are several personalities in the Bible who reflect the same qualities, but Paul stands out. In particular, I am referring to the stirring account of the shipwreck in Acts 27:13–26.

Championship-Level Confidence

Paul had been arrested in Jerusalem for preaching the gospel and was sent to the Roman headquarters in Caesarea where he waited in prison for trial. Being a Roman citizen, he decided to appeal his case in person to Caesar and was shipped out with other prisoners across the Mediterranean Sea to Rome.

Part of the way through the journey—against Paul's warning—the ship's captain set sail at the wrong time and ran into a hurricane-sized storm that threatened to destroy the ship and all its passengers.

When the situation looked hopeless, Paul stood up in front of the bewildered men and shouted to them above the sound of the raging storm, "I urge you to keep up your courage . . ." (Acts 27:22). He went on to tell them that none would lose their lives, even when the ship was destroyed. He told them that an angel of the Lord had come to stand beside him in the night and told him not to be afraid. This angel had informed Paul that he would stand trial before Caesar and that God had graciously given him the lives of all who were sailing with him. "So keep up your courage, men," Paul yelled out, "for I have faith in God that it will happen, just as He told me" (Acts 27:25). Paul's confidence in the Ruler of winds and waves infused him with the boldness to take over as the champion of the hour and persuade the others to hold on.

The shipwreck adventure represents some valuable principles of championship confidence. Let's explore them together.

1. PUT YOUR TRUST IN THE RIGHT PERSON

Paul's life coach was Jesus. He kept in close touch with the One he'd met on the road to Damascus. Whatever Paul accomplished—and it was a lot—was the result of the presence and power of Christ in his life.

Paul reminds us that all we need is found in Christ. He is the Alpha and Omega and all the letters in between. He is the same yesterday (the historic Christ), today (the indwelling Christ), and tomorrow (the returning Christ).

Because of Jesus, I am one of the most blessed men in the world. Four generations of my family before me trusted in Christ; my mother, grandparents, and great-grandparents raised me in the "gospel of parenting according to Jesus." That legacy has continued: Donna and I raised our children to become the fifth generation to put their confidence in Jesus, and now Jefferson, our grandson, is following in the footsteps of his parents, Todd and Julie, who are training him to put his trust in Jesus.

You may not have the Christian heritage backing you up; however, one great thing about trusting Christ is that a new heritage can start with you.

2. BUILD YOUR LIFE ON THE RIGHT PRINCIPLES

The Paul who stood on the deck of that storm-tossed ship was an expert in the Scriptures even before he met Jesus. After his conversion he went off by himself into Arabia to study and meditate with Genesis, Isaiah, and Psalms in his head. After three years, he came out of Arabia with Romans, Ephesians, and the rest of his epistles in his heart. He put principles of the faith down in writing, and we are privileged to have them in our guidebook today.

When I face any given day, I can walk out with confidence knowing that my life choices and leadership decisions can be gauged by a compass that will always steer me in the right direction.

3. KEEP THE RIGHT PERSPECTIVE

When everybody else on the sinking ship was ready to jump overboard, Paul gave them a good dose of heaven-sent optimism. The angelic messenger had told him exactly what to do and what not to do, and that considerably changed the perspective on the situation. It's amazing to me that the Roman guards and crew took Paul's advice, but by doing so, they found out the truth of what he said. Their perspective was their salvation from disaster.

I was fascinated when I heard the story of Kayla Burt, a star basketball player on the Washington Huskies team. When Burt was with her friends at a New Year's Eve get-together, she suddenly fell off the couch where she was watching TV. When her friends checked her, she had stopped breathing, and her face had turned purple. They administered CPR until the paramedics arrived. She was then rushed to the hospital; it turned out that Kayla has a rare heart condition. Fortunately she survived but not without a new perspective on life.

In an ESPN interview she said, "My life will never be the same. In the light of what I just experienced, the things that seemed important to me are no longer important. This made me realize what is important now."

To have the confidence of a champion each day is not something that comes naturally. Our enemy is hell-bent on keeping us fearful and timid in all our endeavors so that God's work is hindered. Yet, if we commit ourselves to following the right coach and maintain the right training regimen and the right attitude, we will preserve championship confidence in everything we do.

You are more than a champion
through our Lord Jesus Christ.

—ROMANS 8:28 (COACH)

CHAPTER FIVE

Hang with Champions

I ADMIT IT; I AM AN OLYMPICS JUNKIE. AT THE 1996 OLYMPIC Games in Atlanta, I watched Michael Johnson win the 200- and 400-meter races and Carl Lewis win the long jump, and I ate lunch with the Dream Team. I also ventured to Salt Lake City to watch the Winter Games. I love the excitement of being in the stands when our athletes win their events.

When I can't be physically present at the games, I am glued to my television. I sit in my living room, cheering for our champions as if I were there. I get so inspired by the athletes' performances; they prepare for years to compete against the greatest athletes in the world. I get incomparable joy from watching them win. For most, it is the greatest feat of their professional careers. I just can't get enough.

During the 2004 Summer Olympics, I watched our US swim team win the final event of the 400-meter individual medley, setting a new world record. What an exciting experience to watch those guys cheer on their teammates with great enthusiasm.

Michael Phelps should have been at poolside, cheering with his team; instead he was in the stands, having given the spot he earned to teammate Ian Crocker. Ian set the world record in the butterfly stroke, and Michael aspired to reach the same goal. In fact, Michael told reporters that he kept a picture of Ian in his room so he would remember to wake up each day and give training his best effort. However, when Michael was given the opportunity to compete on the individual medley team, he gave up his spot. I thought his decision was remarkable and spoke well of Michael's heart and the value he placed on his team.[1]

One particular thing I've always noticed from watching Olympic champions is that they look to other champions for inspiration. Champions want to hang around other champions. In many cases, they move across the country to train together. They know other champions will keep them at the top of their games.

Romans 8:37 says, "You are more than a champion through our Lord Jesus Christ" (COACH). One of the ways we ensure this characteristic comes through in our living is to hang with other champions of the faith. If we are going to live the champion's life that God ordained for us, we've got to understand the value of teaming up with other people who are pursuing God with all their heart.

There are three specific ways teams produce confidence:

1. TEAMS INSPIRE US TO DO OUR BEST

Olympic divers Laura Wilkinson and Kimiko Soldati understood this concept well. Laura was the gold medal winner in the 10-meter platform in Sydney, and Kimiko found inspiration in Laura's character and poise. In preparation for the 2004 Olympics, she called Laura to ask if she might train with her. Laura agreed, and the two trained side by side and eventually earned spots on the 2004 team. When Kimiko made the team Laura said, "I think I was more excited when she made the team than when I did."[2]

Something more valuable came from their relationship as well. Laura is a committed Christian, and during their time training together she was able to lead Kimiko to Christ. After a series of difficult circumstances in her own life, Kimiko had noticed the peace and unconditional joy in Laura, and she asked Laura to share the source. This allowed Laura to explain her relationship with Jesus Christ. Soon after, Kimiko began her own relationship with the Savior.

2. TEAMS INSPIRE US TO REACH FOR THE BEST

Teammates push us to keep improving and to strive to a higher level. Lenny Krayzelburg had been the world-record holder in the 4x100 individual medley for a long time when Aaron Piersol asked him if they could train together. In preparation for the 2004 Games, the two put in long hours together and it eventually paid off. In the first heat at the Olympics, Aaron Piersol set a new world record.

After the race in which he also beat his famous training partner, the two swimmers were interviewed by NBC. Aaron admitted that he wouldn't be half the swimmer he was if it wasn't for Lenny.

3. TEAMS HOLD US ACCOUNTABLE TO BE OUR BEST

Olympic gymnast Paul Hamm won the gold for the men's individual all-around for the US in 2004, but the win didn't come without a lot of ups and downs. After he fell on the vault and scored a 9.137, everyone thought he was out of the competition at twelfth place. Amazingly, he came back in the last event on the horizontal bars to score a 9.837 and win the gold by the narrowest margin in Olympic history.

In the stands cheering Paul on the entire way was his twin brother, Morgan. Their father later told reporters that Paul's win was largely attributed to Morgan's influence. They have fed off each other ever since they were little boys training in the barn by their house. They continually pushed each other to be their best and, as a result, Paul was victorious.

Teaming Up Produces Confidence

When I coached football, I made it a priority to spend time with other coaches who had won state championships and college national championships. I knew I would learn from and be inspired by their habits and success. There was something they were doing that was different, a cut above, and I wanted it.

When I graduated from high school in 1964, I thought I was a pretty good player. I had been an All-State running back and an honorable mention All-American. I was sure I could handle playing at the college level. However, I was not prepared for what I was about to face.

Many of the upper classmen had just returned from a tour in Vietnam, and they were the biggest, ugliest bunch of men I'd ever seen. Hitting a 275- to 285-pound man who had been hardened in the jungles of Vietnam is a little bit different than hitting a 250-pound high-school graduate. To top it off, it was understood that freshmen were open game, and it was hunting season. The upper classmen had a goal to see how many freshmen they could kill and drive off the team. We were dropping like flies.

To make matters worse, it was hot and humid, and they didn't give us any water in those days. They about killed us. In one practice, I lost thirteen pounds of water weight because I was so dehydrated. When they allowed us some water, they brought it in a bucket with ice and a towel. You were supposed to take the towel out of the water and suck on it. But because I was a rookie, I was at the end of the line. All those big burly linemen with dirt all over them had plunged their hands in that water and sloshed the wet towel to their faces. By the time I got my hands on the bucket and peered inside, I wanted to puke. A thought crossed my mind at that practice that had never crossed my mind before: I wondered if I was going to make it. Doubt flooded me as I hung my face over the murky waters in the bucket below me.

Right then, the coach got his whistle and commanded us to line up for sprints. We were all exhausted; we could hardly breathe, and we had to get in place for 40-yard wind sprints. I staggered around, wondering if I could make it. Then out of nowhere, Charley walked up beside me, hit me on the leg, and said, "Hey Rookie, run with me."

I was astounded. He had spoken to *me* . . . and he knew my name, "Rookie." Suddenly, I was energized and confidence began to well up in my heart. I got my hand down alongside him, and wherever he ran, I ran. When he walked, I walked. When he jogged, I jogged.

Charley was an All-American senior fullback, and as a veteran, he knew how to pace himself through hot, demanding practices. Every practice after that, I positioned myself right next to Charley when it came time for wind sprints. He held me accountable and made me better than I would have been alone. He would not let me slack off in any area. He kept reminding me to keep pressing on, that I was going to make it and perform well.

By the time the season started, I not only made the team but I landed a starting position. I knew I owed it to Charley; before he stepped alongside me, I had been thinking I wasn't going to make it any further.

The principle is so simple that we often take it for granted. When we don't pay attention to the people we surround ourselves with, we often pay the price. We lack confidence and lack the tools to give God our best. Yet, God created us to be in relationship with each other. He created us to need each other. If we desire to be champions of faith, we should find champions of the faith who will inspire us to do our best, reach for our best, and daily be our best. These are the people we should be around. Team up with champions today and see your confidence move up to a new level.

Let's consider how we can
inspire one another to live
and love on a higher level.

—HEBREWS 10:24 (COACH)

CHAPTER SIX

Get Tough

WHEN I WAS YOUNG, I PLAYED WHAT WAS KNOWN AS "LITTLE Pro Football." It involved little guys running around, learning to play ball in full pads, making full contact. I'll never forget the first time I had the wind knocked out of me. I remember lying there, gasping for air, trying to inhale. I started to panic. My coach looked at me struggling to catch my breath and muttered, "Come on, Son, you're okay. Get out there and get tough." That was it. No mercy, no pity— just a hand to stand me up and nudge me back out there.

Even my own mother didn't always show me mercy or let me "sit out" on life. In high school, I remember waking one morning with my back in complete spasm after an injury I sustained in a game the night before. I couldn't move. Typically, I pumped gas every Saturday at the local Sears Automotive Center, but this week my plan was to stay in bed and recoup so I could be my best for practice on Monday.

"Mom," I moaned, "I can't work today. I hurt my back." She smirked, and I knew I was getting nowhere. I tried again.

"Mom, I can't move. I can't even bend over to put my pants on." She turned and walked out of the room. A minute later she came back with my work pants in her hands. She leaned over me and began to dress me as I stared at her in disbelief. Once I was dressed, Mom haphazardly rolled me out of bed and walked me outside.

As we approached the car, I tried one more time, "Mom, I can't sit. I can't even bend down to get in the car." She looked at me sternly as she turned me around and stuffed me into the car with my chest on the front seat and my backside facing the window.

When we arrived at the gas pumps, she came around the car, opened my door, pulled me out, and patted me on the back. I just stood there, incredulous. As my mom ducked back into the car, she smiled. "Son, get tough," she said. Then she drove off.

My mom and my coaches taught me an invaluable lesson in my early years. They taught me to never quit. I look back at those experiences and am glad everyone pushed me to persevere. It has made me the person I am today. Toughness is not an easy lesson to learn; pain is never a pleasant experience, but it forged character that pushed me to persevere in any circumstance.

My coaches used to say, "We're going to get all the quit out of you." Their strategy was to make practices harder than any game we would ever play so that by game time we would never be tempted to give up. They certainly accomplished what they set out to do in me; I never tried to quit again. The lesson also carried over into other aspects of my life. Circumstances no longer dictated my resolve. This mindset prepared me for the real storms of life that would inevitably come my way.

At some point, we will all have the wind knocked out of us. We will get hit square in the chest by life's circumstances. How we respond depends on whether or not we possess a spirit of perseverance and spiritual toughness—a no-quit attitude—that will get us through.

If anyone in the Bible could identify with enduring difficult times, it was Paul. He was shipwrecked, jailed, beaten, stoned, and left for dead. Yet to the Corinthian believers, he declares, "For our light and momentary troubles are achieving for us an eternal glory that far outweighs them all. So we fix our eyes not on what is seen, but on what is unseen. For what is seen is temporary, but what is unseen is eternal" (2 Cor. 4:17–18). Paul understood how to maintain a persevering spirit in all circumstances.

How can we attain the same spirit of perseverance? Hebrews 12:1–3 gives us a good game plan. There are three ingredients:

1. LOOK UP FOR INSPIRATION

Verse one begins, "Therefore, since we are surrounded by such a great cloud of witnesses . . ." In other words, the men and women of great faith who have gone on before us are our models of inspiration. We can draw inspiration from their faith, tenacity, and determination. While there are certainly many inspirational "witnesses" spoken of in the Bible, there are often as many in our daily lives.

I have what I like to call an "accountability corner" in my office. On a corner bookshelf, I keep the photographs of five men who have profoundly impacted my life. The first two come from my own family: my grandfather and my great-grandfather. My great-grandfather was a circuit-riding preacher who left a legacy of faith for our family. Likewise, my grandfather served as a preacher his entire life. Both inspire me to carry on our family heritage of service to the Lord.

Dr. Bill Bright, the late founder of Campus Crusade for Christ, is the third photo. I was blessed to know Dr. Bright personally and to be a part of his vision to train pastors and Christian leaders around the world through the Global Pastors Network. Another photo is of Dr. Billy Graham, who once shared with me that his greatest ambition was to "be faithful to the end." He is a true testament of perseverance.

The final photo in my accountability corner is of Reverend Brooks Linn. In 1967, Donna and I served as summer youth pastors at his church in South Florida. Brooks believed in me, encouraged me, and helped to shape my vision to start Christ Fellowship Church. I wouldn't be where I am without him.

Each day I look at these photos and I am filled with a sense of awe. Their faithful witness inspires me to persevere and holds me accountable to carry on the legacy of their lives.

A young man by the name of Steve Saint understands this well. He was working at a successful business when he received word that his aunt had died. The news meant that his family's decades-old ministry would come to an end. There was no one left to see the vision through.

The ministry began back in the 1950s when Steve's father, Nate Saint, and five other men, including Jim Elliot, set out by plane to reach a remote tribe of Auca Indians in Ecuador. All five men were killed along a riverbank. Amazingly, Steve's mother and some of the other widows stayed in Ecuador to carry on the ministry. The Saint family continued the work Nate had started until Steve's aunt was reunited with the rest of her family in heaven.

When Steve considered his family's sacrifice and perseverance over many years, he was persuaded to leave his successful business to carry on the work in the jungles of Ecuador. To this day, Steve is overseeing the ministry because of the inspiration of those who had gone before him.[1]

It is wise to draw inspiration from those in our immediate circles and those outside it—people like Steve. It is important that we surround ourselves with a cloud of people who will draw us closer to God and urge us on, no matter how difficult things get. Often, our witnesses are the main reason we are able to finish the race set before us.

2. LIGHTEN UP THE LOAD

Hebrews 12:1 also tells us to "throw off everything that hinders." Have you ever watched *The Strongest Man Alive Contest* on television?

Burly men from all over the globe compete in a series of strength-testing events for the title of "World's Strongest Man." One of the events requires them to strap into a harness and pull a tractor-trailer. Whoever pulls it the longest distance in the shortest amount of time, wins.

When I watched the event, it brought to my mind numerous believers who are still trudging through life with a truckload of hurt, pain, and disappointment behind them. It's no wonder so many of us get worn out. We need to lighten our loads. To be effective, Paul knew that we had to lay down what was behind us—no matter how heavy—and move toward what was ahead.

Paul spoke from experience, having had a truckload of pain and regret. He assisted in the murder of Stephen, one of the first Christian martyrs. He stood by while this godly man was stoned to death for his faith. When Paul repented and gave his heart to the Lord, he determined to let go of the cargo that weighed him down.

Early in life, Fanny Crosby chose to let God carry her load. When she was still a small girl, she developed a severe eye infection that was mistreated. As a result, she lost her sight. But she never allowed anger or self-pity to hinder her pursuit of God. Instead, she maximized her other senses by memorizing most of the Bible and writing songs of praise. She would eventually write some nine-thousand hymns, including "Blessed Assurance" and "To God Be the Glory."[2]

Fanny Crosby chose to run the race God marked out for her with resolve and perseverance, and her legacy continues to touch lives. We have the same choice to make for ourselves. Will we throw off all that hinders God's work in and through our lives?

If we have sin in our lives, we must confess it to God, and He will unhitch the trailer of guilt, shame, or regret. "If we confess our sins," the Apostle John wrote, "He is faithful and just to forgive us our sins and to cleanse us from all unrighteousness" (1 John 1:9

NKJV). We have a choice in the matter. Will we carry our own burden or let God take it for us?

3. TIGHTEN UP OUR PRIORITIES

"Let us fix our eyes on Jesus," Hebrews 12:2 begins, "the author and perfecter of our faith." This simply means our priorities should reflect the priorities of Christ. His vision, His heart, and His example have to become our passion and pursuit. A focused life is a strengthened life.

Norman Riggs was a stout, strong man who had a smile that would light up a room. You would never imagine the suffering he had endured. While fighting in WWII, he was captured by the Japanese and taken to China, where he was placed in a concentration camp and forced to work in the local mines. There, he literally sat out the rest of the war, deteriorating and losing hope.

One by one, Norman saw his friends die of malnutrition, hypothermia, fatigue, and sickness. He held his best friend in his arms as the man took his last breath. Norman became a skeleton of the strong soldier he once was. Finally, one day in desperation, he took the little shovel he had used to dig in the mines and buried the handle of it in the ground, intending to impale himself on the blade. He couldn't go on another day.

As he was about to plunge his frail body onto the blade, a ray of light broke through the gray skies. As we talked, he recalled the events:

> I couldn't explain what happened, but suddenly in that moment, the light of heaven hit me and warmed me. I knew God was there and that He cared and loved me. A calm peace came over me, and I chose not to take my life that day or ever. Every time I felt the gnawing pangs of hunger that we suffered with every day, I would think about the light of heaven and it would somehow satisfy my

hunger. Every time I was weary and didn't know if I could take another step, I thought about the light and knew God was close to me, giving me the strength to carry on. Every time despair would try to envelop my soul in the darkness of night, I would think about the light of heaven, and it gave me the hope to hold on for one more day.

When troops liberated the concentration camp, they could not believe Norman was alive. Miraculously, he had gained weight on the same rations that had left the other prisoners malnourished.

Yes, the light of heaven broke through the dark skies for all of us on a hill called Calvary. There, Jesus Christ gave His life for us, taking the evil of the world upon Himself. Through His resurrection, He made that light available to all of us. When it seems like all hope is lost, His light will warm us and give us miraculous toughness to press on. His light reminds us that, in spite of our "momentary trials," we are destined for victory. Remember, perseverance develops spiritual toughness that gives us confidence to keep pressing on to victory.

James 1:2–4 says, "Consider it pure joy, my brothers, whenever you face trials of many kinds, because you know that the testing of your faith develops perseverance. Perseverance must finish its work so that you may be mature and complete, not lacking anything." As we get tough in Christ and persevere through trials, we will reach a level of maturity and completeness in Christ that we can not attain on our own and we will lack no good thing.

Romans 8:28 has always been a life verse for me. It gives me great confidence that ". . . in all things God works for the good of those who love him, who have been called according to his purpose." I know that in whatever situation I find myself, in the end it will work for good so I keep my eyes of faith focused on the promise that I will make it through in Christ. Let's get tough in Christ!

Let us not become weary
in doing good, for at the proper
time we will reap a harvest
if we do not give up.

—GALATIANS 6:9

CONFIDENCE IN SELF

CHAPTER SEVEN

Mistaken Identity

HE WAS A SHOE SALESMAN WHO COULD BARELY READ. HE certainly wasn't a natural speaker, and when he was asked to read from the Gospel of John in Sunday school, he flipped through the Old Testament to find it. Dwight L. Moody was one of the most unlikely, unqualified prospects—and yet, in God's time, he became one of the world's leading Christian spokesmen.

God led him to establish a Sunday school in Chicago that thousands began to attend. All the while, Moody remained in the shoe business. It wasn't until he began to receive speaking invitations from various American cities that he stopped selling shoes and became one of history's most influential evangelists. At the age of seventeen, when he was a clerk in his uncle's shoe store, if you had asked Dwight L. Moody who he was, his answer would've fallen well short of the person God would eventually make him to be.[1]

Strength in Weakness

Gideon was another man unsure of his identity. He was threshing wheat in a wine press out of the sight of the Midianites when an angel of the Lord called him "mighty warrior." (I can't help but wonder

when Gideon heard "mighty warrior" if he looked around for someone else in the room.) At the time, Gideon was fearful, and he was
hiding from his enemy. These details didn't matter. God saw his
potential and called him to something great.

In the same way, our current circumstances never cause God to
lose sight of our potential. He sees us for who we can be. He knows
what He has planted in our hearts and minds.

When God called Gideon, he immediately began making
excuses. "But Lord," he said, "how can I save Israel? My clan is the
weakest in Manasseh, and I am the least in my family" (Judges
6:15). In other words, "Lord, surely you are aware that I am not
known for my leadership, nor am I known for any great exploits. We
don't have any *Calebs* or *Joshuas* in our clan. We are just not capable
of taking on an assignment like this. And just one more thing, Lord,
in my family, I'm the least qualified for this. There is no way I can
pull this off."

Isn't it amazing how we sometimes react when God lays out a
challenge before us? It's all too typical of us to step back and start
justifying why we can't or shouldn't or really don't have the time. I'm
glad God wasn't deterred by Gideon's excuses. "Gideon, here's the
deal," the angel said. "God has placed a hidden strength in you. He's
stored up unknown talents and abilities in you that you don't even
know about yet. They are going to be revealed as you serve and obey
Him" (Judges 6:14 COACH).

Gideon took the angel's word for it and began to make prepara-
tions to lead Israel into battle. When 32,000 men showed up to
fight, the Lord whittled the group down to the three hundred men
who knelt on one knee and took the water in their hand and lapped
it up to their mouths (Judges 7:6).

Put yourself in Gideon's shoes. You have sheepishly stepped up,
you are ready to take the plunge and battle a much bigger and stronger

army at God's command, and then He asks you to do it with only a small fraction of your resources. I'm sure Gideon had his doubts—but he kept moving forward. Now God would unfold the plan.

Gideon instructed the men to hold their trumpets and hide their torches in jars so no one would see the light until he gave the command to break the jars and shine the lights. The men followed Gideon's orders, and the Lord startled the Midianites so thoroughly that they turned on each other (Judges 7:20–22). When it was all said and done, the entire Midianite army was dead, and Gideon's three hundred troops gathered all the possessions of their enemy.

The victory produced two key outcomes: the great oppression of the Midianites was lifted off of Israel and they enjoyed peace for forty years, and spiritual balance was brought back to the nation. Here's what Gideon told the people in Judges 8:23: "I will not rule over you, nor will my son rule over you. The LORD will rule over you." The nation had been restored to their true Leader.

There was one more outcome. Gideon was blessed when all the soldiers brought a portion of their wealth that they had captured from the enemy and gave it to him as a gift. Gideon certainly didn't go into the situation to prosper—he may have initially hoped to merely survive—but he came out of it blessed because he learned a simple principle that day: when you honor God, He will always honor you. There are three lessons we learn from Gideon's story to have greater confidence in ourselves in God's sight:

LESSON #1: STOP HIDING OUT

We've been hiding way too long. We can try to fly beneath the radar, go about our daily lives unnoticed, and be satisfied with our small doses of spiritual encouragement. But if we're going to live a life of impact and make a difference, we've got to get in the game.

When Franklin Graham, evangelist Billy Graham's son, reluctantly preached a sermon for the first time in his life, not one of the thousand people in attendance responded to the gospel invitation. Franklin swore that he would never preach again. For the following six years, he resisted invitations to preach. Finally, his friend, John Wesley White, persuaded him to stop hiding from his call to preach. White recounts Franklin's return to the pulpit at a rally in Juneau, Alaska: "They packed the place, drunks and prostitutes. [Franklin preached,] gave the invitation and they poured down. It was a miracle, and he knew it."[2] Franklin came out of hiding that night, and for more than fifteen years he has seen tens of thousands come to Christ through his ministry.

LESSON #2: STOP MAKING EXCUSES

It's amazing how quickly we make excuses. This indicates, more often than anything, our unwillingness to move outside our creature comforts. We like things to be predictable and safe, and when something or someone calls us out, our knee-jerk reaction is defensiveness. But often the only thing God is asking of us is a willing heart. How often do we feel ill-equipped for a task before us? I'll be the first to admit, it happens fairly often. But I've learned that when I don't know how or what to do, God just wants my willingness to obey.

It wasn't about how well Gideon's troops played the trumpet that threw the Midianites into frenzy; it was the fact that they were merely willing to blow into those trumpets and make a loud noise. Whenever God finds a heart that is willing to obey Him, He will do great things. Remember that God knows what He's placed in us. He knows exactly what our abilities, talents, gifts, and hidden strengths are; He will reveal those if we will step up and say, "I am willing. Show me what to do."

In his book *An Unstoppable Force*, Erwin McManus discusses his experience growing as a new Christian. After his decision to follow Christ, he was faced with another altar call, a calling to lordship. A few weeks later, there was another altar call, a calling to the ministry. After that, two more calls: a calling for home ministry and a calling to foreign ministry. He was having a tough time getting all of these calls straight in his mind. He explains the conclusion he reached:

> Paul seemed to think there was only one calling. He writes to Timothy, "So do not be ashamed to testify about our Lord, or ashamed of me His prisoner. But join with me in suffering for the gospel, by the power of God, who has saved us and called us to a holy life—not because of anything we have done but because of His own purpose and grace." (2 Tim. 1:8–9)[3]

I believe the Scriptures seem to simplify the process of calling. Our one call is to willingly lay our life at the feet of Jesus and to do whatever He asks. His calling is always consistent with His Word, and He will always call you into something that will bring value to others. God's calling always shapes you more into the character and nature of Christ.

LESSON #3: STEP INTO GOD-FOCUS

Stepping out of self-focus and into God-focus will radically transform your life. Gideon walked out of the mundane and into his destiny when he was willing to serve God unconditionally. It wasn't his first reaction but it was his eventual decision—that's the most important thing.

One way to remain in God-focus is to serve others. When you serve others, you keep in step with the Spirit of God (Gal. 5: 25). You capture the heart and attitude of Christ. What did Jesus do before He was taken to the cross? He washed the feet of His disciples and left them this one last lesson of service. In essence, He said, "You'll reach your destiny if you learn this principle of washing each other's feet." It was not just about the physical act, it was about the attitude of the heart to say, "What can I do to serve my brother?"

A well-known English minister, Henry Varley, once told Dwight L. Moody, "The world has yet to see what God will do with and for and through and in and by a man who is fully consecrated to Him."

"He said, 'a' man," Moody later wrote. "He did not say a 'great' man, nor a 'learned' man, nor a 'smart' man but simply 'a' man. I am 'a' man, and it lies with the man himself whether he will or will not make that full consecration. I will try my utmost to be that man."[4]

What would God do in us, and in the world, if we all came to the same conclusion?

It is time we take our torches out of the jugs and start blowing our horns. God will do the rest. Seeing ourselves as God sees us produces true self-confidence. The closer we draw to Jesus, the more we discover our identity.

> Remain in me, and I will remain in you.
> No branch can bear fruit by itself;
> it must remain in the vine. Neither can
> you bear fruit unless you remain in me.
>
> —JOHN 15:4

CHAPTER EIGHT
Fear to Faith

AFTER FLEEING EGYPT, MOSES SPENT FORTY YEARS IN THE wilderness. He married and raised a family, until one day he came across a bush that was burning but not consumed. The Lord called to Moses from within the bush, commanding him to stay where he was and to take off his sandals. God told Moses that He was concerned about the suffering the Israelites were facing under the hand of the Egyptians. He wanted to use Moses to lead them out of that land into the Promised Land.

Although Moses' first response was one of fear, God did not allow that impulse to change His plan. God does not want us to be controlled by fear either; rather, He desires us to step boldly down the path that leads toward the purpose He has for us. The path may be littered with obstacles, but we must overcome in order to seize our destiny in Christ. Moses had to overcome three obstacles steeped in fear in order to fulfill God's plan. They are common to many of us.

OBSTACLE #1: OVERCOMING HIS PAST

Moses had a rough past—one he would've liked to forget. He once killed an Egyptian for abusing a Hebrew slave. Moses thought no one saw him, but he was eventually discovered and forced to flee

(Ex. 2:11–15). Still, God chose to use Moses—baggage and all—to rescue His chosen people (Ex. 3:7–10).

Some of us have pasts we don't want to face. On top of that, the enemy will use these bad or shameful memories to cripple us. Fortunately, God loves to use people with mixed up, messed up pasts. Consider the apostle Paul, who wrote thirteen books of the New Testament and was one of the greatest missionaries in Christendom. Jesus Christ's ministry notwithstanding, Paul presumably impacted more people's lives than anyone in history. But the apostle Paul was an imperfect man, a murderer like Moses. Thankfully, God is in the habit of transforming broken people for His purposes. God is into stories of redemption.

Knowing this, we should not allow the enemy of our souls to use anything in our past to keep us from the future God intends for us. Be open to His ways, realizing that you are a new creation in Christ (2 Cor. 5:17). Remember that when we enter into a relationship with Jesus, embracing His work on the cross, our past is wiped clean. This is a promise. We may still have to suffer the consequences of wrong choices we made, but in God's eyes we are forgiven. The beauty of grace is that it has no memory.

Norma McCorvey knows this well. She was a drug addict who had two children out of wedlock, whom she gave up for adoption. When she got pregnant a third time, she couldn't bear the thought of giving up another child, so she sought out an illegal abortion. The Dallas clinic, however, had been raided and shut down. Not knowing what to do, she made up a story that she'd been raped and signed an affidavit on condition of anonymity, and a lawsuit began.

Advocates for a woman's right to choose got a hold of Norma and gave her the name "Jane Roe." Two green, self-serving attorneys used her as their star witness in the landmark case *Roe v. Wade*. As a result of Jane Roe's made-up testimony of rape and her subsequent inability to have an abortion, the Supreme Court legalized abortion on demand in our country.

Soon after the ruling, Norma was working at a Planned Parenthood abortion clinic when Operation Rescue moved in next door. A seven-year-old girl named Emily, the daughter of an O.R. worker, visited Norma regularly and openly showed affection for her, despite Norma's past. Over time, Emily's consistent love softened Norma's heart until she began to comprehend Christ's love for her. Finally, she accepted Emily's invitation to attend church with her family. There, Norma McCorvey—the infamous Jane Roe—repented of her past and gave Christ her heart. Not long after, she began a ministry called "Roe No More," which continues to fight today for the rights of unborn children.[1]

Once the poster child for the pro-choice movement and an enemy of God's purposes, Norma McCorvey is now fighting for the lives of millions in our country. Her story reiterates that no matter how far away you are from Him, God can and will use a repentant heart surrendered to Him.

OBSTACLE #2: OVERCOME PRESENT COMFORTS

Moses was about eighty years old when God called to him from the burning bush, so he probably wasn't very interested in major changes to his lifestyle. Yet, God had more for him to do. As long as you have breath, God will use you.

As soon as God presented the task to Moses, he began making excuses. It takes great faith and courage to step out of a secure lifestyle. However, real growth rarely takes place until we are willing to step outside our comfort zones. As we do each day, God can unlock a new experience to learn from. Our part is simply to remain open to His call.

I recently read a story about a small-town preacher in Pennsylvania.

His church of fifty coalminers and farmers grew to about two hundred through his leadership. This preacher, however, grew comfortable in the church's success as the Lord abundantly blessed his ministry.

Then one evening, he was reading a *Time* magazine article about a destructive gang in New York City. His passion for the gospel was ignited once more, and he decided to travel to the city and help however he could with the gang problem. He stumbled around the streets and subways, trying to make a difference even though he didn't have a clue where to begin. In fact, the people back home began urging him to return home, unconvinced that his presence was making any impact on the problem. The preacher persisted, though, and eventually began holding crusades. He built relationships with a group of teenagers who were hooked on drugs and helped them overcome their addictions and come to a saving knowledge of Jesus. The experience compelled the preacher, Dave Wilkerson, to form an organization called Teen Challenge, which today helps drug-addicted teenagers all over the world.

Eventually Wilkerson moved his family to New York and started a small church there. Years later, Times Square Church in downtown Manhattan ministers to thousands each week.[2] Because this small-town country preacher was willing to step out of his comfort zone into the unknown, God used his life immeasurably.

OBSTACLE #3: OVERCOME INSECURITIES

When God called Moses, Moses quickly pointed to his inadequacies. "Whoa, wait a minute; who am I that I should go? What will I say to them? Suppose they don't believe me. I'm slow of speech. Please send somebody else" (Ex. 3:11, 4:1–13 COACH). Moses was looking at himself instead of God. In a mirror of insecurity, he saw all his weaknesses and failures and thus felt ill-equipped to do what God was asking him to do.

Thinking we have to work out all our weaknesses before we can do anything great for God is a common mistake. In everyday life, we learn to first fix the flat and then drive the car. But this is not how God works. As long as we remain willing to be used, we are exactly where God wants us. He will do any repair work that is necessary and use us both during and after it is complete. The truth is that if we waited to be "fixed" before we made ourselves available to God, we'd never be available.

God desires that our confidence in Him not fold when life circumstances seem insurmountable—the kind of confidence that acknowledges (but not justifies) weakness as an opportunity for God to show His strength and glory, the kind that doesn't lay out excuses but rather is humbled at how God uses people like us to accomplish great things.

If we live in fear, our faith is hobbled, often to the point of complete ineffectiveness. Fear paralyzes us. But God wants us to run toward the obstacles in our path, relying on His strength to propel us over, under, around, or through them. We can't let the obstacles of our past cripple our future. Neither can we let our present comforts make us complacent. Our insecurities will not stop God from strengthening us. His strength is our confidence.

> So we say with confidence, "The Lord is my helper; I will not be afraid . . ."
>
> —Hebrews 13:6

CHAPTER NINE

Recovering Our Fumbles

I was asked to speak at a federal prison in Jesup, Georgia. As I prayed about what to share, I felt strongly about telling the story of Jonah, a man who had completely turned his back on God and eventually hit rock bottom.

As I stood up to share, I quickly recognized a man sitting in the front row with a sullen look on his face. This man, who had also hit rock bottom, was none other than Jim Bakker, the notorious televangelist. Caught up in the PTL scandal, he was now a broken man, and I knew then that God wanted him to hear the message that I had prepared: we serve the God of second chance.

At the end of the message, I gave an invitation for men to come forward who wanted to receive another chance from God. I told them God was willing to reach out to them and to love them, forgive them, and give them a new hope. Many men accepted the challenge.

The first man to make his way up the aisle towards me had an extremely serious look on his face as he stared straight ahead. I couldn't interpret from his body language what he was thinking or feeling until he got closer and I saw tears start to fall down his puffy cheeks. He stepped closer and fell into my arms. "Coach, I have messed up so bad."

Through our conversation, I learned that this young man knew who I was because he once played on a rival football team. He actually knew some of the players that had played for me. The young man related well to some of the stories I shared in my message, and his heart was touched to share with me some of the tragic mistakes that landed him in the Jesup prison.

I looked him straight in the eyes, gripped his shoulders and said, "Son, I'm so glad that I'm here tonight to give you some good news. You serve a God who is famous for giving us a second chance. If you are sincere in your heart, and will turn to Him, He will truly touch and transform your life." The young man found a new hope that night.

After the crowd dispersed, Jim Bakker approached me. With tears falling, he began to recount all the mistakes and poor decisions he had made. He brought to light all of his flops, fumbles, and failures. He was caught in deep regret and loneliness. Pain flowed from every word.

In that moment, I looked at him, and all I could think about was how God worked in Jonah. "Jim, aren't you glad we serve the God who is willing to forgive honest hearts that turn to Him?" Jim returned a weak smile and asked to pray with me for God's healing in his life.

No matter how unconfident, unsure, and unworthy we've come to feel, God desires to be with us and to shower us with His love and forgiveness. Most of all, He desires to restore in us confident hearts in Him. Jonah's testimony touched the hearts of many men that night in Jesup, Georgia, and I believe it can touch our lives as well, on a big or small scale. I find three keys in Jonah's life that teach us how to remain confident in God on the heels of life's inevitable flops, fumbles, and failures:

KEY #1: RECOGNIZE FAILURE AND KEEP IT IN PERSPECTIVE

At times we take ourselves way too seriously and fall into pits of self-pity, thinking we will never be able to get back out again. We eventually bury ourselves in despair and defeat. The thing to remember is that our failures don't have to be our tombstones; they can be stepping-stones.

A story is told of a farmer who had a mule that fell into a well. The farmer thought, "Well, there is no way I can get that old mule up out of there so I'm just going to bury him in this well." He got on his truck and began dumping loads of dirt on that old mule. Each time a load fell on him, the mule would kick and squirm around in the well until he got above the dirt tossed on him. Eventually the mule was able to step his way to the top of the well and step out of the well and onto ground.[1]

You see, the mule saw the piles of dirt as stepping-stones to safety. He had the right perspective and it saved his life. Imagine what would happen if we were determined not to give up no matter what life dumps on us. As men and women of faith, we refuse to allow the fear and disappointment of our failures to rob us of faith in God's ability to overcome them. Yes, we have to accept responsibility in our areas of failure but we also have to learn how to use the stepping-stones of life to grow and, ultimately, refocus on God's plan.

If you know the story of Jonah, you know that God called him to go and be His spokesperson to the wicked city of Nineveh. Instead of obeying the call of God, Jonah headed in the opposite direction. He hid on a boat headed for Tarshish.

While at sea, a great storm arose. The shipmen feared for their lives and began throwing cargo overboard to keep the ship afloat. When they found Jonah sleeping in the bottom of the boat, they woke him in a panic. Jonah realized what was happening. He had disobeyed God, and the storm was a result of his disobedience. He said, "Pick me up, and throw me into the sea . . . and it will become calm. I know that it is my fault that this great storm has come upon you" (Jonah 1:12).

Every choice we make has an influence on someone around us. Our failures especially impact those closest to us. Jonah finally understood this and he accepted responsibility for his failure.

The men tossed Jonah into the raging sea to die. However, God sent a great fish to swallow Jonah and to preserve his life while God worked on his heart. Scripture tells us, "From inside the fish Jonah prayed to the LORD his God" (Jonah 2:1). Jonah's time of reflection within the fish leads us to our second key.

KEY #2: REACH UP TO GOD

God is always reaching out to us. Jonah not only recognized his failure, but also he called to God, and God replied. Why is it that when we fail, we often try to hide from God and make things right through our own efforts? Does that make sense when it was our own actions that got us into the mess in the first place? God is the only one who can truly bring good out of a bad situation. We need to run to Him when we've messed up. Proverbs 18:10 says, "The name of the LORD is a strong tower; the righteous run to it and are safe." When we reach up to God, He strengthens and assures us.

In the 1988 Olympic Games, British sprinter Derrick Redmond tore his hamstring and collapsed in the 400-meter finals. Four years later, in Barcelona, he was a favorite to win the race. As he rounded the final turn, something popped and he fell to the track, writhing in agony. He had torn his hamstring again. As the other racers crossed the finish line, Redmond struggled to hobble toward the finish line. He stood for a second; then he fell again. Judges surrounded him and tried to escort him to the side, but he insisted on finishing the race.

Suddenly, from the stands, an older man started darting toward the track. He broke through security and ran toward Redmond. It was the sprinter's father. When he reached his son, he held out his hand and helped Redmond to stand. He placed his shoulder beneath

Redmond's arm and acted as a crutch. Together, the two began walking toward the finish line and completed the race.[2] Our Heavenly Father does just the same. He is watching us, coaching us, rooting us on to victory. It doesn't matter how many times we fall; He never fails to run to us and offer His hand to lift us up and His body to steady us. If we reach back to our Father, He'll lead us to the finish line.

KEY #3: MAKE CHANGES NECESSARY FOR OBEDIENCE

"Then the word of the LORD came to Jonah a second time . . . Jonah obeyed the word of the LORD and went to Nineveh" (Jonah 3:1, 3).

After repenting, Jonah reengaged his original mission from God. He did not let his failures distract him from his mission. God honored Jonah for his willingness to go, and an entire city was saved.

We, too, need to treat failure as a teacher. Thomas Edison is a good example of this; he failed on more than a thousand experiments before finally inventing the light bulb. Many shook their heads at him and asked, "Thomas, aren't you discouraged?" He said, "I am not discouraged because every wrong attempt discarded is another step forward."[3] Failures are something we can learn from.

John Maxwell wrote in his book *Failing Forward* that when life knocks you down, learn something from your failures so that when you get up, you will not trip over them a second time.[4]

Failures should never get in the way of fulfilling our destiny. Baseball great Babe Ruth understood this well. He struck out 1,330 times, yet he held the all-time home run record.[5] Likewise, Hank Aaron, who ended up beating Babe Ruth's home run record, struck out 1,383 times.[6] Despite their many mistakes, both of these men became legends of the game because they didn't let their failures destroy their dream of being the best.

Philippians 1:6 says, "Being confident of this, that He who began a good work in you will carry it on to completion until the day of Christ Jesus." In other words, don't get down about your faults and weaknesses. We are not defined by our mistakes and failures but rather by our identity as children of God. We are coheirs to the throne, and our King promises us that persevering in our faith—learning from our mistakes along the way—gives us confidence for our new beginnings. Remember, we serve the God of the second chance.

> So do not throw away your confidence;
> it will be richly rewarded.
>
> —HEBREWS 10:35

CHAPTER TEN

Heads Up

I RECENTLY RECEIVED NEWS ABOUT A MINISTER WHO HAD an affair with one of his staff members. As a result, his marriage was destroyed, his church shattered, and his reputation tarnished. Our enemy is real, and he wants nothing more than to rob us of our destiny, kill our dreams, and destroy our lives (John 10:10). It's important that we protect ourselves from his plots to harm us.

When he was a young preacher in Middletown, Ohio, my grandfather received a phone call from a woman, pleading with him to come to her house to discuss an urgent prayer request. Grandpa, a faithful pastor, husband, and father to four children, hurried off to make the house call for prayer.

When he arrived and knocked on the door, the woman who had called for him appeared in the doorway dressed in her negligee. Clearly the woman had other intentions for his visit. Grandpa backed up so quickly that he nearly fell off the porch. "Please come in," she called to him. Instead of stopping to entertain the idea or even answering her, he ran for the car and didn't look back.

Years later he recounted to me, "Son, I learned an important lesson that day; never go to visit anyone—especially a woman—alone. Jesus sent the disciples out by twos because we need a covering at all times." As a result, I've made it my personal practice to protect myself and my staff by demanding a covering when we counsel or visit with those of the opposite sex. I always prefer having my wife present when I am counseling with another woman. We never want to be unprotected in a moment of temptation from the enemy, so we build in safeguards. In considering how to best do this, we should consider the lives of two great men of faith in the Bible and how they each handled temptation differently. Hopefully, we can learn some valuable lessons from their examples.

Responses to Temptation

As we have already seen, both Joseph and David were men of faith. Both were men who intended to honor God. But when it came down to it, they reacted very differently to temptation.

Joseph refused the offer of Potiphar's wife, a woman who was undoubtedly beautiful and certainly powerful and unaccustomed to hearing the word *no*. She repeatedly tried to seduce Joseph when Potiphar was away, and he continued to refuse her . . . until finally, he had to run away from her (Gen. 39).

David's story is quite different. David was a strong man, a warrior, and a man who loved God deeply—but he couldn't resist a moment of vulnerability. We're told that from his terrace, David took in Bathsheba's beauty; his gaze turned to lust, and in a moment of weakness he asked his servants to bring her to him. That night he committed adultery with her.

To make matters worse, when David found out she was pregnant, he put together a plan to cover up his affair; a plan that intentionally placed Bathsheba's husband Uriah on the front lines of battle where he was killed (2 Sam. 11).

When you compare the two stories, a subtle difference becomes

clear. David was vulnerable because he left himself open to temptation. He was supposed to be on the battle lines with his troops but
he stayed behind by himself. Still, this wasn't the only reason for his
downfall. He still had opportunity to avoid sin when he first noticed
Bathsheba bathing. He could have turned away and gone back
inside—avoided an accidental glance turning into a lustful gaze.
Instead, David entertained the temptation and ultimately couldn't
get loose from its grip.

On the other hand, when Potiphar's seductive wife tempted
Joseph, he refused to compromise. He wanted nothing to do with the
situation, and ultimately, he removed himself from the temptation.

In the end, Joseph relied on God and David relied on himself.
We are often fooled into thinking that our strength will sustain us—
especially if God has given us favor and a privileged position. But
ultimately, we are no battle for the enemy. This is why Paul gives us
both a warning and a promise:

> So, if you think you are standing firm, be careful that you don't fall!
> No temptation has seized you except what is common to man. And
> God is faithful; he will not let you be tempted beyond what you can
> bear. But when you are tempted, he will also provide a way out so
> that you can stand up under it. (1 Cor. 10:12–13)

STAY ALERT

We need to keep our eyes open. Vulnerability can be masked as
confidence in the flesh. Paul reminds us that the only way we can have
confidence in the midst of temptation is by looking to God, putting
our faith and trust in Him alone. God will provide a way out so that
we can stand with confidence against temptation. Look for the door;
there will always be a door leading to freedom. Joseph found that door,
and it helped preserve his testimony. David never looked for it.

STAY IN FELLOWSHIP

Eventually, God sent a man named Nathan to confront David, and David confessed his sin and asked for forgiveness (2 Sam. 12). In Psalm 51:10, David prays, "Create in me a clean heart, O God, and renew a steadfast spirit within me" (NKJV).

If we give in to temptation, the tempter will try to use guilt to weaken us and to keep us from making things right with God. But we should always remember that God is a God of mercy and grace. He wants to forgive us and make us whole again. Staying in fellowship with God is especially critical after a fall. It deflects the enemy's arrows of guilt and shame and quietly builds our confidence in the Holy Spirit who strengthens us.

Additionally, we should surround ourselves with men and women of faith. If David had his mighty men with him, I can guarantee you he would not have fallen to temptation. As I told you earlier, I have strong men of faith around me that I can run to during the trying times of life.

Accountability is a needed part of our lives, but there will still be times when we must face temptation alone. It is in these times that God must be enough. If we are near to Him, His strength will see us through.

STAY FOCUSED

If we are to resist the enemy, we should first recognize that he is real and then remember, ". . . greater is He who is in you than he who is in the world" (1 John 4:4 NASB). Ultimately, this is our confidence in the midst of temptation. It doesn't mean, however, that we shouldn't take precautions ahead of time. We need to foster our relationship with Christ when temptation is not present. That way, when temptation comes, we are trained and ready to respond properly—we will follow the footsteps of Joseph and not David.

Here's the key to confidence in the face of temptation: Guard your heart, and your heart will guard you. We must keep our hearts sensitive to the heart of Christ. When we are driven with the desire to honor Christ in every way, we will always build safeguards into our lives. These safeguards include guarding what we allow to dominate our minds, our eyes, and our time; carefully considering who we associate with; being honest about our strengths and weaknesses; and allowing others of faith to speak openly into our lives. Guard your heart and your heart will guard you.

Above all else, guard your heart,
for it is the wellspring of life.

—PROVERBS 4:23

CHAPTER ELEVEN

Confidence in God's Covenants

COVENANT IS NOT A COMMON WORD TODAY. IN BIBLICAL times, covenant was a part of the everyday life. When two people made a covenant with each other, they would often seal that covenant or agreement by taking a sandal off and actually hitting it against the ground (or giving it to the other person as in Ruth 4:7) as a sign of commitment.

We can have real confidence in our covenant with God. Such covenants usually involve three main elements:

1. Covenants always bring understanding of God's commitment to us, and God's desire for us to be committed to Him.

2. Covenants focus on relationships—those we have with God, and those we have with one another.

3. Covenants have a purpose. God has a distinct purpose for everyone with whom He enters a covenant. When we understand the elements of a true covenant, this will birth in us a greater sense of security and confidence to face the challenges of life.

CHARACTERISTIC #1: COMMITMENT

My wife and I had the honor of visiting Billy and Ruth Graham in their home in North Carolina. Dr. Graham has always been one of my heroes of the faith, so to be able to sit and talk with him and his wife about their lives and their years of fruitful ministry, all while sipping on root beer floats, was an extraordinary experience.

One thing in particular that really struck me during our visit was Dr. Graham's humility, balanced with a passionate desire to be faithful to God to the very end of his journey.

Billy and Ruth Graham are people of covenant. They understand commitment and faithfulness to God and to His call upon their lives. As a young preacher, Dr. Graham made a pivotal decision when a friend challenged him regarding the reliability of the Word of God. One evening during a walk in the San Bernardino Mountains, he took hold of his Bible, dropped to his knees, and made a covenant that he would believe and preach the Word of God until he died.[1]

The impact of Billy Graham's covenant that night is still yet to be fully known. The countless millions of lives that have found freedom and confidence in life through Christ are unknown. His ministry of God's Word to the nations is unprecedented.

Covenant is about a commitment like Dr. Graham's. Without such commitment, we will never fully experience the confidence God desires for us to know in our lives. Covenant is always about honoring God's purpose for your life through your commitment to His ways.

CHARACTERISTIC #2: RELATIONSHIP

Dick and Mable Smith are two major reasons that our church flourishes today. We can trace our beginnings to this amazing couple whose unconditional love touched the lives of those who began Christ Fellowship. In essence, Dick and Mable acted as an extension of God's covenant with Abraham; they shared God's love with others and their ministry continues to branch out today, increasing exponentially every year our church grows. What was once only a handful of people is now a church of more than twenty thousand—thanks to the covenant two people made to foster loving relationships. The impact of our lives is in direct proportion to the level of our commitment to God. The greater our commitment to His will and purposes, the greater the impact we will have on others for eternity.

God did something similar in the life of Abraham and it is the reason we now call him "Father Abraham." When Abraham was ninety-nine years old, Scripture says that God appeared to him and confirmed a covenant that He would greatly increase Abraham's family (Gen. 17:1–2). He did this to demonstrate His commitment to a love relationship with His people. Later, God tested Abraham's love for Him—He wanted to see whether Abraham was serious about his side of the deal. God asked him to sacrifice his son Isaac in order to prove his commitment.

Abraham had confidence that God had a bigger purpose in this request and that He would never ask him to do something contrary to His perfect will. He obeyed God and tied Isaac to an altar to sacrifice him. In that moment, God knew that Abraham was committed to the covenant they had made. He spared Isaac and fulfilled His promise to Abraham by making him the "father of many nations" (Gen. 22).

CHARACTERISTIC #3: PURPOSE

Earlier in this book we discussed how Moses, a former prince of Egypt, fled his hometown after committing murder. God then called on him to set the children of Israel free from the tyranny of the Egyptians. In doing so, God entered a covenant of purpose with Moses saying, "Now if you obey me fully and keep my covenant, then out of all nations, you will be my treasured possession. Although the whole earth is mine, you will be for me a kingdom of priests and a holy nation" (Ex. 19:5–6).

God purposed to make the children of Israel a privileged empire, set apart to welcome the coming King who would reign over the entire world one day. He then dispatched Moses to become His hands and feet and to carry out this purpose.

A covenant with God offers us a higher calling. God then equips us with the necessary gifts and talents to see this purpose through. In covenant with God, He will fulfill the destiny that He has planned for us as we remain obedient.

I am inspired by the life of Watchman Nee, a Chinese Christian who remained committed to God even as he suffered in a communist prison. Eventually he died there. From those who knew him, we are told that he didn't complain or condemn others, but concentrated on the calling and purpose of witnessing for Christ right up to the moment of his martyrdom. His covenant with God defined his purpose for life.

In his writings that remain with us, Nee observes:

> No one can voluntarily offer up all he has on the altar if God has not first appeared to him. By nature, no one can offer himself to God. Even when a man does want to offer himself to God, he finds that he really has nothing to offer . . . When man meets God, consecration takes place spontaneously in his life. If you catch sight of God just once and touch God just once, you are no longer your own. God is Someone who cannot be touched lightly! Once a man touches God, he can no longer live for himself.[2]

Covenant Breakers and Covenant Keepers

You may remember the story; Pharaoh would not agree to let his slaves, the children of Israel, go free. God kept putting plagues on

Egypt after Pharaoh remained defiant. Finally, God told Moses that He was going to send the death angel over all the homes in Egypt. All of the firstborn children and animals would die unless they had the blood of a sacrificed lamb on their doorframes. God would spare all those who had the sign of covenant on their homes.

Pharaoh's firstborn son was among those who died when the death angel passed over. He summoned Moses and told him to gather God's people and leave his country (Ex. 7–12).

This event became known as the Passover, which is still celebrated today. It was a wonderful symbol of the new covenant God would form with His people by sending Jesus to die for our sins, bringing us back into relationship with God. Christ Himself became the mediator of a new covenant between God and us.

Have you ever heard of a mezuzah? It is a small container with a scroll inside, found on the doorposts of many Jewish homes. On the scroll are the words of Deuteronomy 6:4–9. The presence of a mezuzah in one's home is an outward declaration that the home honors God. The mezuzah symbolizes that the home is built on a foundation of commitment to God, relationship with God, and the purposes of God. Even if we don't have a mezuzah hanging on our doorframe as a physical symbol, we can still have the same foundation for our homes.

Forty-one years ago, Donna and I entered into covenant together before God. Our marriage has thrived this long because we are faithfully committed to seeing our marriage vows through every season of life together. Whenever I honor and rejoice in the wife of my youth (Prov. 5:18), it rekindles something in me, prompting me to be the best husband I can be for her. I want to keep building my life, my marriage, and my ministry on a covenant of commitment because I know God will be honored. He will pour out His favor and blessing on our marriage and our ministry as we honor and love Him.

Donna and I also strive to develop God-honoring relationships in our home. When we are in regular communion with Jesus, our relationship is much healthier. In fact, the health of all of our other relationships is contingent upon the health of our relationship with God. A right relationship with God translates into healthier relationships with everyone in our lives.

God desires to be in covenant with us. We are created for covenant. It is the stabilizing factor in any longstanding relationship. Have you entered into a covenant with God or your family? Don't let another day pass without fortifying your foundation. Stand solid on your commitment, love, and purpose. As you do, God promises to keep you strong in the midst of tough times and pour His favor and blessing into your life and the life of your family. Eventually, He will tell us, "Well done" for having kept our covenants (Matt. 25:23).

For the eyes of the LORD range
throughout the earth to strengthen
those whose hearts are
fully committed to him . . .

—2 CHRONICLES 16:9

CONFIDENCE IN RELATIONSHIPS

CHAPTER TWELVE

Homes of Honor

THE UNITED STATES MARINE CORP'S MOTTO IS *"SEMPER Fidelis,"* which means "Always Faithful." I think of that motto as a type of honor code. Marines are notoriously committed to their country and to their fellow soldiers, willing to give up their lives in service whether they are wearing fatigues on the battlefield or their blues as civilians. Once a Marine, always a Marine.

I believe we should have a similar honor code in our homes, a code of commitment to our God and to our families. When we live with this commitment, we can have the confidence that God will honor our homes. In fact, this is one of the reasons Paul wrote, "He [Christ] is before all things, and in Him all things hold together" (Col. 1:17).

Families disintegrate because they don't allow Christ to be the center of their homes. It seems that many attempt success on their own, but eventually discover that without Christ at the center, a home can quickly fall apart. We need to allow Him to be the stabilizer. Through Him, we can know and experience the fullness of God's love, goodness, mercy, power, and authority in our family relationships and endeavors.

What does a home of honor look like? The definition of *honor* in the Greek is to prize, value, and revere. When God is in the center of our homes, we prize Him, we revere Him. We also prize, value, and revere each other. I believe there are three indicators that reveal whether or not our home is upholding this code of honor:

INDICATOR #1: HOMES OF HONOR HAVE ACTIVE FAITH

"And without faith," says Hebrews 11:6, "it is impossible to please God, because anyone who comes to him must believe that he exists and that he rewards those who earnestly seek him."

This might be the most important indicator of a home of honor. It's so easy for us to become casual in our faith. We often measure our moral and spiritual success by the world's standards. As long as we're living better than those around us then we are fine; but that's not the point. The real issue is whether we are passionately pursuing God and obeying Him each step of the way.

The natural outcome of passionate faith is a prosperous home life. Jesus says He came to give us abundant life (John 10:10). This abundance at home takes the form of prosperity, or health and vitality, in our relationships with Him and with one another. This is the promise of Proverbs 21:21, which says, "He who pursues righteousness and love finds life, prosperity and honor."

Pray together. One of my greatest joys is praying with my grandson, Jefferson. He has such a tender heart towards God. Recently, I was traveling back from a speaking engagement when I decided to call home and check in with my family. Jefferson happened to be at our house and answered my call. After talking with him, he prayed for my traveling safety over the phone.

What a treasure. His actions are the direct result of our family working hard to create a culture of prayer in our home. We cover our conversations in prayer; it isn't something embarrassing or awkward, just natural. Prayer with our children, at any age, is something we recognize that we desperately need in our home.

After talking with many men over the years, I've come to realize that husbands find it difficult to pray with their wives. This is unfortunate because praying with your spouse is a great way to deepen your intimacy with her. Most men don't realize that praying doesn't have to be long or eloquent. It can be as simple as a short prayer before you head out in the morning or during the day in the form of a call, e-mail, or even a text message. Donna and I share in short prayers like these because we realize that prayer changes things; most importantly it changes us.

Our prayers include thanksgiving for each other, strength and integrity in our work, and blessings for our families. Our prayers include the things in life we hold precious—our families and each other.

Praying together doesn't have to be complicated. We should just be honest before God and one another. Commit your day to the Lord's will and direction and see how it will affect the entire tone of your household. Even if you live alone, find ways to fill your home with prayer. Whether it's calling a friend or involvement in a small group; be purposeful about your prayer life.

Read God's Word together. Another way to instill passionate faith into our homes is to place high value on the Word of God. Openly studying and sharing the Bible at home not only gives us God's perspective on life and direction for the journey together, it also indicates our reliance on it for daily decisions. This is why Deuteronomy 6:6–7 says, "These commandments that I give you today are to be upon your hearts. Impress them on your children. Talk about them when you sit at home and when you walk along the road, when you lie down and when you get up." As parents, it is our responsibility to nurture and grow our children. Our homes should be growth centers where everyone feels encouraged to increase in their understanding and love for God.

Worship God together. Worship is another marker of a passionate faith. Worship music should fill our homes. Praise and worship helps set a certain tone, allowing our hearts to focus on God's heart.

One evening, after a family dinner at our home, we were sitting around chatting when Jefferson announced, "I think we need to have church." He proceeded to lead us in a song, the reading of Genesis 1:1, and prayer. I remember sitting and talking with Donna that night and tears came to our eyes as we discussed how beautiful it was to see that our precious grandson felt free to worship God in our home. Genuine worship starts in the place we rise up each morning and lay our heads each night.

INDICATOR #2: HOMES OF HONOR LIVE FOR GOD'S PURPOSES

We were created by God, for God (Col. 1:16). God created us for several reasons: to live with purpose and meaning, to worship and please Him, to be in fellowship with Him, to know how to be in right relationship with one another, and to grow together toward eternity with Him. Namely, God created us for Him, to honor Him. Our homes should reflect a commitment to this purpose.

One day after a Sunday service, a woman walked up to me and said, "I'm the bug lady who sprays the interior and exterior of your son Todd's house. I was spraying the other day for bugs and needed a signature to prove I had been there, so I asked Jefferson if he would like to sign his name. He said, 'Okay, but I want to tell you something first before I sign. I prayed to receive Jesus Christ as my personal Savior.' I guess he wanted to be sure that I knew Jesus as well."

In his heart, Jefferson wanted to make sure that the bug lady also knew Christ personally; he understood that sharing the Good News was a part of God's purpose for him. I am not saying that before we sign for every package we should say, "Hey, I just want you to know that before I sign for this, I happen to know Jesus." However, people who come in contact with us should be able to tell that Jesus is in us. Our lives should speak of His love and grace and compassion. It should be obvious to people who enter our homes that our top priority is Christ and His purposes. Young Jefferson knew that sharing his life was important; it was part of his purpose and that flowed from him without apology.

The important thing to remember is to put God first in our homes. This may translate differently from family to family in terms of practicality, but our promise is the same. God says "Those who honor me, I will honor" (1 Sam. 2:30). When we "seek first His kingdom," He will add to our homes all that we need (Matt. 6:33).

INDICATOR #3: HOMES OF HONOR HAVE PEOPLE WHO HONOR EACH OTHER

"Do to others what you would have them do to you" (Matt. 7:12). The verse, which sums up all Jewish law and the words of the prophets, is the foundation for what we often call *The Golden Rule*. The rule simply boils down to this: speak to others the way we want to be spoken to, treat others the way we want to be treated, and respect others the way we want to be respected. To put it another way, when we honor others, we honor God.

Marines understand this well. They value honor because they know that a soldier who holds honor in high regard values the lives of other people. A sacrificial attitude is their standard. And at the heart of honor is service. In the same way, a God-honoring home serves the people in it. In fact, each day we should look for ways to show those in our home how much we value them, by affirming them in various ways. It could be as simple as offering a kind word or taking time to do something subtle that demonstrates our love for them.

There are other ways we can build a home that honors God, but any list would not be complete without the three indicators we have just discussed. Homes that foster faith, further God's purposes, and seek to honor one another are fundamentally honoring to God. They will not only be safe within His protection and provision, they will receive the blessings of God's kingdom now and later. Expressing the love our homes desire and demand will bring confidence to our entire family.

. . . Those who honor me I will honor . . .

—1 Samuel 2:30

CHAPTER THIRTEEN

Confidence with Communication

IS YOUR LIFE BECOMING TOO "VIRTUALLY CONNECTED," OUT of control with technology? I recently came across a list that offered some telling signs[1]:

- You have a list of fifteen phone numbers to reach your family of three.
- You call your son's cell phone to let him know it's time to eat. He e-mails you back from his bedroom, "What's for dinner?"
- Your daughter sells Girl Scout cookies via her Web site.
- You chat several times with a stranger from South Africa but you haven't spoken to your neighbor yet this year.
- Your reason for not staying in touch with family members is that you do not have their e-mail addresses.
- You consider second day airmail painfully slow.
- You hear most of your jokes via e-mail instead of in person—and when you receive a good one, you are more likely to forward the e-mail than tell the joke at the dinner table.

This commentary on modern-day interaction is sadly accurate. While communication is the fuel that drives relationships, one main thing that seems to be causing our relationships to sputter is our inability to effectively communicate as God designed.

Regardless of their complexity, all communications have five basic elements:

1. What you think you want to say,
2. What you actually say,
3. What the other person thinks he/she heard you say,
4. The other person's response to what he/she heard you say,
5. Your reaction to his/her interpretation of what you said.

With all this confusion, it's easy to see why we have so much trouble communicating.

I believe our problems may have originated in the Garden of Eden. I have my own theory, of course: When God created Eve, we know He took a rib out of Adam and formed Eve with it. Unfortunately, the center of communication control must have been located in that removed rib; as soon as it was gone, man suddenly lost his ability to communicate effectively. In turn, Eve was gifted with the ability to communicate.

If you want to test this, put a three-year-old girl and boy in the middle of a group of adults and see what happens. The little girl will talk to you, whereas the little boy will do little more than grunt and make car noises. (When they get older, women continue this pattern and men change their noises to sighing and snoring.)

Whether or not my humorous little theory is correct, it is certainly true that communication is an essential part of both men's and women's lives, whether or not we're confident at it. This becomes doubly true when we consider that Jesus entrusted His disciples, and all Christians who followed, with the responsibility of communicating to the world the Good News of His victory over death.

Clearly, communication is vital in the fulfilling of our commission and the fruitfulness of our relationships. This is why Paul writes, "Let your conversation be always full of grace, seasoned with salt, so that you may know how to answer everyone" (Col. 4:6).

When I read that verse I think of Martin Howe, a dear Jamaican pastor on our staff. Whenever Martin meets someone, he always pronounces a blessing on that person. Every time I see him, I head straight toward him because I love to receive his blessing. Who doesn't enjoy the company of somebody whose words are full of grace and blessing?

Being a gracious, effective communicator like Martin allows us to connect with people and, ultimately, to foster authentic relationships. This then gives us opportunity to share the world's greatest story, Jesus Christ, and the world's greatest gift, love. Therefore how well we communicate and relate is vital; in light of this, let me give you four important communication principles:

PRINCIPLE #1: BE THOUGHTFUL IN YOUR SPEECH

"Do not let any unwholesome talk come out of your mouths," exhorts Ephesians 4:29, "but only what is helpful for building others up according to their needs that it may benefit those who listen." That word "unwholesome" in the Greek means anything that could hurt, tear down, or affect somebody else in a negative way. When we communicate, we should always consider the needs of others, how to encourage them, and how to help build their faith.

Consider the story of Charles Dickens. His life did not provide him the conditions to become a great writer, yet he was inspired to continue pursuing this vocation through the thoughtful communication of one man.

Forced to quit school when he was twelve due to his father's imprisonment, Dickens spent his days pasting labels on bottles in a rat-infested workplace. He pursued his dream of writing in his spare time, only to have his work rejected time and time again. But one day, in yet another rejection letter, an editor included a note telling Dickens he was a great writer, and the world needed him. These thoughtful words sent Dickens rejoicing up and down the streets of London.[2] They also served as staying power in a career that produced literary masterpieces such as *Oliver Twist, Great Expectations, A Tale of Two Cities,* and *A Christmas Carol.*

I believe the only way for us to consistently achieve thoughtful communication, both in what we say and how we say it, is for everything that springs from us to be first bathed in the Spirit of God. By allowing the Holy Spirit to be the wellspring of our communication, our words will be coated in kindness, gentleness, goodness, mercy, and loaded with God's love.

PRINCIPLE #2: EFFECTIVE COMMUNICATION MUST ALWAYS BE HONEST

We need to get back to where our "yes" really means "yes" and our "no" simply means "no" (Matt. 5:37). Proverbs 24:26 expresses this idea in a very interesting way. It says, "An honest answer is like a kiss on the lips." I think I understand this comparison. I always enjoy kissing my wife, and I delight in the fact that our kiss contains the assurance of trust and honest vulnerability.

Reporting in *USA Today,* Jerald Jellison asserted, "Each of us fibs at least fifty times a day." He explained that we lie about our age, our income, or our accomplishments. And we use lies to escape embarrassment. A common reason for "little white lies," we're told, is to protect someone else's feelings. Aren't we really protecting ourselves? Jellison went on to detail what he considers our most commonly used fibs:

- "I wasn't feeling well."
- "I didn't want to hurt your feelings."
- "The check is in the mail."
- "I was just kidding."
- "I was only trying to help."[3]

Wouldn't it improve our relationships all around if we were simply honest with one another? It would certainly be a refreshing change. Let's be honest with each other every day—with a loving tone and motive behind everything we say to one another.

PRINCIPLE #3: EFFECTIVE COMMUNICATION REQUIRES EFFECTIVE LISTENING

The art of listening escapes many of us. Several years ago, I was interviewing one of our pastors for an end-of-the-year evaluation. I began the interview by asking, "What, as a leader, can I do to help you be more effective in your ministry?"

Brian Benjamin, whom I was interviewing, looked at me and said, "Well, Pastor, you could learn to be a better listener. When I'm talking to you, you seem like you are always distracted and you look at your watch. You interrupt me a lot because you run ahead of my conversations." I went home and told Donna, expecting some sympathy. "Honey," she said, "I've told you the same thing." I learned a valuable lesson as a leader: stop talking so much and start listening more often.

PRINCIPLE #4: EFFECTIVE COMMUNICATION TAKES TIME

Learning to communicate has never been a top priority in American society, and it may be far less so today. The average teenager watches twenty-one hours of TV a week yet spends less than five minutes a day dialoguing with his mother and father.[4] Many couples spend less than *four minutes* in meaningful conversation a day.[5] How often do husbands grab the remote control and start clicking while their wives are dying to talk with them? If you want to rack up some points, men, turn it off right in the middle of something they know you want to watch and say, "Honey, can we just talk for a moment?"

To become effective communicators, we need to appease ourselves far less frequently. When we turn our want-meter off and show others that we are genuinely interested in what they have to say, we show them they matter to us. Our relationships deteriorate often because we are so infatuated with our own stories and agendas.

On the other hand, when we take time to listen to others and open ourselves to them, we begin to gain confidence and clarity in relationships. We begin to weave threads through the lives of others, and they weave threads through ours. In the end, the greatest benefit of effective communication is the ongoing experience of deep, meaningful relationships with the people in our lives and with our God. Nothing is more significant. Effective communication builds confidence into our relationships.

Do not let any unwholesome talk
come out of your mouths, but only
what is helpful for building others up
according to their needs, that it
may benefit those who listen.

—Ephesians 4:29

CHAPTER FOURTEEN

The Power of Forgiveness

On December 20, 1974, ten-year-old Chris Carrier was walking home from school when a man pulled up in a van. The man opened the door and convinced Chris to come with him to help plan a party for the boy's father.

Chris was just a few blocks from home when he excitedly hopped in the van for a trip that would change his life forever. There was no party to plan; instead the man planned to kill Chris to get revenge on the boy's father. He drove Chris to the Florida Everglades where he stabbed him repeatedly with an ice pick. He then dragged the boy out of the vehicle, shot him through the head, and left him for dead.

Six days later a hunter found Chris who, despite his horrific wounds, was still breathing. The young boy miraculously survived, but he lost an eye where the bullet went through his skull.

Twenty years later, a detective came across David McAllister, a man dying in a nursing home, who confessed to the crime. The detective invited Chris to meet David because the man wanted to ask for his forgiveness. Chris, now twenty-six, agreed to the meeting.

As he walked nervously into the room, the first thing he noticed was that the one who had taken one of his eyes was himself completely blind. Chris was overcome with emotion for the man lying there, broken and alone. That day Chris received David's apology and forgave him.

Over the next several weeks, something more miraculous than Chris's survival began to occur. The boy whom David McAllister left for dead began visiting him on a regular basis. Chris shared Jesus' love and grace with him. Eventually, Chris led his former assailant to salvation. A few weeks later, David died and entered eternity in peace.

How Many Times?

"How many times should I forgive my brother who sins against me?" Peter asked Jesus. "Seven times?" Looking at Peter lovingly, Jesus replied that he needed to forgive not just seven times, but seventy (see Matthew 18:21–22).

We can relate to Peter's inquiry today. We have all been hurt at some point in our lives. Sometimes forgiving the one who caused us pain is difficult. Our memories of pain and betrayal, lies and manipulation remain ever-present in our minds.

We harbor these emotions when we aren't willing or don't know how to release them properly. Eventually they swell up in our hearts, causing a tsunami of inner turmoil. It is critical that we learn how to forgive others so we can avoid this imminent destruction. Jesus came not only to set us free from our sins but also the sins of others against us.

So how do we forgive those who hurt us deeply? James 2:13 puts it simply: "Mercy triumphs over judgment." But how can we make this triumph a reality in our lives?

When it comes to forgiveness, we need to guard our hearts so that we continually respond to others in mercy as Jesus did when he said, "Father, forgive them for they know not what they do," (Luke 23:34 KJV). Only the mercy that allowed Jesus to love those who falsely accused and crucified Him will help us to forgive our offenders. God wants us to offer to others the same mercy He has poured over us (Matt. 6:14–15). But how?

Release Judgment and Pain Into God's Hands

"God is just," says 2 Thessalonians 1:6. "He will pay back trouble to those who trouble you." Waiting on God's judgment becomes increasingly difficult in direct proportion to the size of the sin against us. We want immediate results; we want the truth to be known and our pain vindicated. In such emotional times, we can also feel like we're minimizing or justifying a person's offense against us if we release it to God.

However, releasing the offenses to God allows us to rise above them. When we hold on to pain, we become captives to it. Once captive, we fall prey to its negative effects. Our relationships suffer as well as our spiritual lives, not to mention the physical ramifications that come from unresolved pain: stress, anger, anxiety, and depression. Ephesians 4:26–27 explains that if we don't deal with our negative emotions, Satan gains a stronghold in our lives. Anger and unforgiveness are thieves of all that God has intended for us, but God can break the stronghold.

A good example of this is a man I know named Ray. He tried everything to counteract the abusive attitude of his boss but it seemed that even courtesy and generosity couldn't solve the problem. His boss's hostility was directed at Ray because he wouldn't join in the foul language, dirty jokes, and "drinks with the boys" after work. After months of frustration, Ray bowed his head at his desk one afternoon and placed the situation in God's hands. The following day, the boss asked Ray to pray with him about a family situation. God had begun a work in the man's life in direct response to Ray's prayer. Today, Ray and his boss are friends and the staff of their business meets together for prayer at the start of every work-day. If we'll let Him, God can break the cycle of pain, frustration, or anger in our lives and use the situation to draw others to Him.

Unfortunately, there will be times when there is no quick resolution to a particular source of conflict. But even in these situations, God will not abandon us. Sometimes He changes our circumstances. At other times, He uses our circumstances to change our hearts.

Reinforcement Through the Word of God

"Great peace have they which love thy law," says Psalm 119:165, "and nothing shall offend them" (KJV). Wouldn't you love to have such a peace? Wouldn't you love to have nothing offend you? There is no magic formula to the effect of the Bible. When we read it, we don't suddenly become impermeable to insults and painful offenses against us. What happens is that we begin to take on the mind of Christ. Put another way, we begin to forget ourselves and focus on the pain in our offenders that would cause them do such things. We begin to recognize that their need for Christ is the same as ours, as anyone's.

This is one of the reasons Jesus said, "If any man will come after me, let him deny himself and take up his cross, and follow me," (Matt. 16:24 KJV). If we can learn to die to ourselves, we will find that we are no longer easily offended—we will see the situations are not really about us; they are about broken people in need of a Savior. Certainly, we are not going to walk through life without relational problems or heartaches. The difference is that when we learn to focus on God through hurtful times—when we learn to see the situations through His perspective—we will face them with the confidence, humility, and grace of Jesus Christ.

God's Word contains all the power we need to deal with the offensive things this world throws at us. Consider these three tools the Word gives us to deal confidently with the issues of forgiveness in our lives:

1. THE WORD HELPS US TO HAVE THE MIND OF CHRIST

When we see things the way Jesus sees them, we can look beyond the faults of people to see their real needs. We have to be careful not to use this perspective with a condescending attitude. We are no better than our offenders in God's kingdom. The only difference is that they have a need that has not yet been met. We should continually pray that God would fill us with compassion and mercy toward those who offend us so that His work can be done in their lives.

2. THE WORD WILL REVEAL THE TRUTH OF THE ISSUE TO YOU

The Word gives us spiritual discernment to cut through the issue at hand and understand a deeper pain fermenting in the hearts of others. Hebrews 4:12 says, "For the word of God is living and active. Sharper than any double-edged sword, it penetrates even to dividing soul and spirit, joints and marrow; it judges the thoughts and attitudes of the heart."

In other words, the Word will let us see things for what they really are. Friends, we must refuse to let an offense rob us of our joy. Instead, we can turn an ugly situation into something that reveals God's glory, mercy, and loving kindness.

3. THE WORD OF GOD HELPS US TO RISE ABOVE THE OFFENSE AND TAKE THE HIGHER GROUND

We cannot possibly rely on our own wisdom to overcome deep hurts and pain. The Word of God brings the healing we desperately long for in our lives. It takes us to a higher ground where we can readily offer the forgiveness our offender needs from us.

In order to put the crippling emotions of unforgiveness behind us and live in the confidence of a Christ-like attitude, we need to remember that the real enemy is Satan. He is out to destroy us with every power he has available to him. If he can keep us stewing in anger or resentment, he will. We need confidence to know that our mustard seed faith will take us to the higher ground.

If we let God handle our tendency to cast judgment on others, we will find release from the emotions associated with unforgiveness. God is big enough to hold our pain in His hands and release it. Our part is to simply rely on the promises of the Word of God where pain and forgiveness are concerned. We should remind ourselves regularly of the real need in hurtful situations: namely, others' need for Christ. As Chris found, there may be no better way to introduce a person to our Lord than through loving forgiveness in the midst of a painful offense. Forgiveness produces a confidence that will transform us—and others around us as well.

For if you forgive men when
they sin against you,
your heavenly Father
will also forgive you.

—Matthew 6:14

CHAPTER FIFTEEN

Honoring the Dishonorable

IN RESPONSE TO MY FATHER'S DAY MESSAGE, A YOUNG woman approached me, looked me in the eye and asked, "Pastor Tom, how am I supposed to forgive a father who abused me?"

Honoring a person who has dishonored us is one of the most difficult challenges in the area of personal relationships. That's because there is never an excuse for abuse. It cannot be justified, and it should not be tolerated. No one should feel any kind of obligation to remain in an abusive relationship.

When I have preached or taught the biblical commandment of honoring your father and mother, invariably someone comes up to me, tells me about an abusive parent, and relates how hard it is for them to give honor under the shadow of their bad memories. It is important to understand that the solution to this conflict is not found in our own reactive human reasoning. The key to coming to terms with honoring a person who has abused us is to trust that God can work through us in the lives of family or friends who have failed us.

In order for us to live with a confident faith that reflects the heart and mind of Christ, we need to face these issues head-on. The story of David's relationship with King Saul gives us insight into how God expects us to react to those who do not deserve our honor or respect.

The Principle of the Torn Robe

Defeating Goliath won David great fame in Israel as a warrior. We're also told David was an accomplished musician—there is an account in the Bible where King Saul invites David into his courts to play music to soothe his spirit. Imagine David's shock when Saul, enraged with jealousy over David's talent and popularity, tries to pin him to the wall with a spear. This incident began a long battle of cat-and-mouse between King Saul and David.

David lived for years as a refugee in his own land. Accompanied by a band of famous mercenaries, he was just able to stay one step ahead of the jealous, murder-minded king. In one hair-raising episode, Saul and his three thousand soldiers came upon a cave. The king went inside to relieve himself, but he was not alone. David and his men were hiding farther back in the cave. Convinced that the Lord had delivered Saul into their hands, David's men urged David to seize the opportunity and end the game. But instead of cutting the clueless king to pieces, David crept up unnoticed and cut off a corner of Saul's robe.

After King Saul left the cave to rejoin his troops, David came out to the cave entrance, held up the piece of robe, and announced that he had spared Saul's life. The act of mercy proved he was not guilty of rebellion—as Saul had been convinced—and had no intention of killing the king or taking the throne by force (1 Sam. 24).

David did not back down from Saul, but he also refused to react in defense. His response teaches us an interesting principle: genuine confidence in God fills us with love and mercy, preventing us from reacting in self-centered vengeance to "settle a score." This confidence in God allows us to be magnanimous, or big-hearted, in our judgment of others. This "Principle of the Torn Robe" can be difficult to learn—and even more difficult to put into practice. It has three parts:

PART #1: REFUSE TO RETALIATE

"The LORD forbid," replied David to his troops, "that I should do such a thing to my master, the LORD's anointed, or lift my hand against him; for he is the anointed of the LORD" (1 Sam. 24:6).

David's forbearance did not depend on whether Saul's behavior was right or wrong. Politically speaking, David would have been justified had he decided to kill Saul and assume the throne. The reason David did not use his sword to settle matters is that Saul became king of Israel by the anointing of God. In the cave, David honored God's anointing by sparing Saul's life. When David cut off the corner of Saul's garment, it was a sign that Saul himself could have easily been cut off.

There is an ancient Jewish tradition still practiced today that dates back to the time of Moses. When a man dies, before he is buried, he is covered with his own prayer shawl, and one of its four corners is cut off. When David cut off one corner of Saul's garment, it was, in effect, a symbolic move that said, "You could have been dead if I had wanted to take your life. Instead, that is up to God, not me. I have no desire to harm you." Saul would have understood this very well. This is why David cried out to Saul from the mouth of the cave, "May the LORD judge between you and me. And may the LORD avenge the wrongs you have done to me, but my hand will not touch you" (1 Sam. 24:12).

We should follow David's example with an understanding that we have no direct authorization from God to exercise vengeance. We are not empowered to assume worthiness to condemn a man who has been handpicked by God. Even though David was anointed, and Saul deserved to be punished, it was not his call to judge how Saul would be punished; that right is God's alone.

PART #2: HONOR GOD BY FORGIVING AS GOD FORGIVES

"For if you forgive men when they sin against you, your heavenly Father will also forgive you" (Matt 6:14).

Although God exercises justice and judgment on those who rebel against Him, His Word reveals that He is also a compassionate and forgiving God. David experienced God's mercy firsthand after he pursued the deadly affair with Bathsheba. David expressed his deep need and appreciation for God's forgiveness in Psalm 51:1–2, "Have mercy on me, O God according to your unfailing love; according to your great compassion blot out my transgressions. Wash away all my iniquity and cleanse me from my sin." Perhaps this experience with God's great and undeserved mercy is what taught David the discernment to handle the situation with Saul honorably.

We should always keep in mind that what God forgives, He forgets (Ps. 103:12). That is part of His mercy toward us. David must have understood this from the experience with Bathsheba. In this way, forgiveness always triumphs over vengeance. This is why Paul writes, "Be kind and compassionate to one another, forgiving each other, just as in Christ God forgave you" (Eph. 4:32).

PART #3: FIGHT THE RIGHT BATTLE

"For our struggle is not against flesh and blood, but against the rulers, against the authorities, against the powers of this dark world and against the spiritual forces of evil in the heavenly realms" (Eph. 6:12).

There is little doubt that David discerned the torment inside the twisted soul of King Saul. Looking beyond the surface behavior of the paranoid monarch of Israel, David saw a victim of Satan's destructive lies. I believe David determined that he was not going to let the same devilish influence do a number on him as well. He refused to allow resentment, revenge, and an unforgiving spirit to rob him of meaning and effectiveness in his life.

David ensured his own protection from Satan by choosing to take the route of mercy. Although he experienced his share of abuse from King Saul, he had no intention of allowing that abuse and rejection to turn him into a hateful agent of retaliation. I'm certain it wasn't easy for David. The psalms are full of heartfelt cries to God to come to his defense. In one, David asks God how long he will have to run from his enemies. Yet, despite the difficulty, David continually resisted resentment toward those who wronged him repeatedly. Furthermore, he didn't allow the dishonor of others to rob him of his own destiny.

As we allow God's mercy and honor toward us to escort us through the tough terrain where dishonor is rampant, we will develop a strong and durable confidence to face any relational abuse in our lives—even the worst. This does not mean it will be easy; it does mean that with God's help, it is possible. With God, *all* things are possible (Matt. 19:26).

. . . for the LORD will be your confidence
and will keep your foot
from being snared.

—PROVERBS 3:26

CHAPTER SIXTEEN

Real Friendship

THERE WILL COME A TIME IN YOUR LIFE WHEN, NO MATTER how strong or independent you think you are, you will need somebody to lean on. When God created Adam, He recognized this need in him. He subsequently created Eve to be Adam's partner. In this way, God designed us to long for each other in relationship. When we come to the end of our life on earth, what will matter most are those we love and those who love us.

Friendship is the foundation of all healthy, vibrant relationships. The story of David and Jonathan (1 Sam. 20) serves as a great example of true, God-honoring friendship. It provides us with a perfect template for learning how to build lasting friendships with confidence.

When David was on the run from Saul, Jonathan assured him that he would prevent his father from hurting David. This infuriated Saul so much that he even tried to kill his own son. Jonathan then knew that David was in serious trouble, so he went back to warn David to run and hide. The two friends wept together before they separated, and Jonathan reminded David that he could count on him to be his defender.

I've always loved this story because it demonstrates what genuine friendship really looks like. Paul shares the secret to relationships like the one between Jonathan and David in Romans 12:9–10. "Love must be sincere," he writes, "hate what is evil; cling to what is good. Be devoted to one another in brotherly love. Honor one another above yourselves." There are three key ingredients in this passage that are foundational for solid relationships:

INGREDIENT #1: SINCERITY

Have you ever met someone who seemed to be sizing you up, to determine whether you were a person worth knowing? Such people are users. If we enter relationships with others for what we can *get out* of them instead of what we can *add to* them, we will constantly be disappointed and will never be able to cultivate real friendships. An ancient philosopher recognized this when he asserted, "He who looks for an advantage out of a friendship strips it from all its nobility."

Real friends are honest with you, and they encourage you to be honest with them. This level of sincerity provides security. This is precisely why David could run to Jonathan. He knew Jonathan would tell him the truth, even when it wasn't easy to hear. Proverbs 27:6 puts it this way: "Wounds from a friend can be trusted but an enemy multiplies kisses."

I have a good system in place for being honest with my friends. There are three questions I ask myself before I speak:

- Will what I am about to say bring value to them?
- Will I share this with a spirit of compassion?
- Is this issue even necessary to bring up with them?

In the end, the key to having great friends is being a great friend. If you want people in your life that you can trust, you have to be a person they can trust.

INGREDIENT #2: DEVOTION

Friends are not friends just in the good times. Real friends stick by you when life gets tough. In authentic relationships, the adversity builds mutual sympathy—a common passion that binds you together.

Jonathan and David were bound together by their common passion for God and for His will to be done in the nation of Israel. This is why Jonathan gave up his right to the throne. It was quite a sacrifice, but he believed that God had anointed David to be the next king. As a result, he made it a priority to honor David at all times. Both Jonathan and David were focused on God's plans; in doing so, they continually honored one another and their individual roles.

Donna and I are complete opposites, but what binds us together is our common passion for God. When God is our common passion, no matter how opposite we may be from one another, we will have a bond that can't be broken. This principle holds true in all relationships, not just marriage.

Even in the early years of our marriage, when I was totally consumed with pursuing a football career, we made sure we spent every Sunday in a church somewhere serving God together. We made God a priority, and it has paid off. To this day, our common passion for Him enables us to stay devoted to each other for the long haul.

Perhaps your relationships are a mess right now. Stop and evaluate if the reason for this is that the central focus of the relationship is something other than your common passion for God. I believe our Lord can reunite any broken relationship if both people involved are willing to get their focus back on Him and allow Him to lead their daily decisions.

INGREDIENT #3: HONOR

We honor each other as friends when we add value to each other's lives, when we love each other unconditionally and continually look for opportunities to affirm or encourage one another. This is the essence of Ephesians 4:29, which says, "Do not let any unwholesome talk come out of your mouths, but only that which is helpful for building others up according to their needs that it may benefit those who listen."

Encouragement should be the goal of our speech, and we should look for people who have that same goal. Those who don't are likely to betray a confidence (Prov. 20:19).

In addition to honoring others through encouragement, we need to be agents of peace. We read that Jonathan told David, "Go in peace" (1 Sam. 20:42). This is indicative of his confidence in their friendship. The ongoing harmony between them was a foundation for God's work in and through them. The same will hold true for us.

"I no longer call you servants," said Jesus, "Instead, I have called you friends" (John 15:15). Ultimately, our righteous actions and confidence in relationships are an outgrowth of our relationship with Christ. Our friendship with Him leads us in fostering lasting, honoring friendships with one another. His plan is that we would love one another wholeheartedly and give our lives for one another as He has given His life for us. By God's design, friendships provide us greater confidence to walk in His will and carry out the purposes for which He's called us. This is why His Word tells us that "a cord of three strands is not quickly broken" (Eccl. 4:12).

When we understand how to craft cords of true friendship, we are continually equipped to walk in God's will, against the forces of this world with confidence. Our friendships are God's gift to us to support and strengthen us to fulfill His higher purposes for our lives.

A friend loves at all times,
and a brother is born for adversity.

—PROVERBS 17:17

CONFIDENCE IN CRISIS

CHAPTER SEVENTEEN

Don't Look to the Rubble

WE WILL NEVER FORGET SEPTEMBER 11, 2001. I WAS SHAR-
ing breakfast with my staff that fateful Tuesday morning when one
of our assistants came to me and asked me to pray. She had just
heard that a plane had crashed into the World Trade Center. Shortly
after we prayed, I returned to my office and saw the unexpected display of terror on the television. The events of that day left America
standing in a heap of physical, emotional, and spiritual rubble upon
which our nation continues to rebuild.

Your personal life might be in a similar state. You might feel like
you're standing in a heap of emotional wreckage from a shattered
relationship or an abusive past. You may be knee-deep in the rubble
of financial hardship, thinking you'll never be able to dig out. We've
all felt these types of burdens and, in the midst of them, our confidence can crumble. But there is still hope. God offers a plan to take
the rubble in our lives and rebuild something beautiful.

RISING FROM THE RUBBLE

Nehemiah knew a thing or two about rubble. A faithful man
during Israel's Babylonian captivity, he learned that his hometown
of Jerusalem was all but destroyed by its enemies. The city lay in

ruins, its wall torn down, and its gates burned. Nehemiah's heart was broken over the devastation, and he immediately knelt in prayer. In time, he was given an opportunity to return to his homeland, but God had something more to rebuild than the city.

When Nehemiah returned to Jerusalem to survey the rubble and make plans to rebuild, God gave him a greater vision: Nehemiah would rebuild the faith of the people as he rebuilt the wall of his city (Neh. 1–2).

God's plan always entails more than physical labor. While He certainly expects that we act in obedience, His foundational rebuilding plans are about renewing His people. Where Nehemiah was concerned, the rebuilding of Jerusalem was simply an outward manifestation of what God desired to do within the people of Israel. Ultimately, Nehemiah was sent as God's messenger to turn the soul of a nation back to Himself.

With specific instructions on how to rebuild the city, reconstruction got underway. The Israelites, however, became discouraged in the midst of the rebuilding project. The physical task seemed insurmountable, and they lost sight of God's vision for their lives. Focusing on the reasons for the rubble, they feared recurring attacks instead of focusing on the One who could redeem the rubble of their lives (Neh. 4).

CONFIDENCE IN CRITICAL TIMES

"I lift up my eyes to the hills—where does my help come from? My help comes from the LORD, the Maker of heaven and earth" (Ps. 121:1–2).

We, too, have a tendency to lose confidence in God's plan when we see the rubble all around us. Psalm 121:1–2 encourages us to refocus on God, lifting our eyes to Him in our critical time of need. This isn't an easy task.

When Nehemiah heard the grumbling of the Israelites, he knew he had to take action. He divided the people by families, and stationed them by their homes. He then gave them a message of hope with three distinct points:

1. Do not be afraid.
2. Remember how great and mighty the Lord is.
3. Be ready to fight for your brothers, sons, daughters, wives, and homes. (Neh. 4:14)

The Israelites' devastation resulted in fear. Like many of us, they were allowing their lack of confidence to rule their decisions and run their lives. It was keeping them from rebuilding. Sometimes a little reminder is necessary for us to regain the confidence to continue. For the Israelites, it couldn't have been difficult to recall the stories that had been passed down about their ancestors. It hadn't been that long ago that God rained manna from heaven, parted the Red Sea, and spouted water from a rock.

What has God done in our lives? I'm sure that if we sat down together, we could remember many instances where God has come through in a way that only He can. When Philippians 4:19 says, "And my God will meet all your needs according to his glorious riches in Christ Jesus," this doesn't mean that His providence was only good enough for yesterday. He has more than enough for today and tomorrow.

The remnants of pain and heartache are difficult to understand. But we don't have to understand pain to move beyond it and rebuild. In fact, we will probably not understand much of the rubble in our lives until later, in some cases not until we are in heaven. In this lifetime, in an effort to draw us to Him, God asks us to strive to know Him better because He knows that when we understand more and more of His character, we will doubt Him less and less. There is no perfect formula for rebuilding other than submitting our plans to God. He works in redemption and His tools are ones of the soul. He knows that rebuilding a life begins on the inside, no matter how harsh the outside circumstances might be.

When it comes down to it, the process of rebuilding is a battle that our enemy will fight against. His work is in creating rubble and if he can keep us in it, he will. This is why Jeremiah acknowledged that the Israelites should prepare to fight. There were certainly physical battles to come, but the most important battle was for their hearts. Jeremiah knew that if God ruled their hearts, they would win the battles against the rebuilding process.

It is likely that Paul considered the Israelites when he wrote his letters to the Ephesians, another group of believers who needed their confidence restored. In order to fight, Paul says we must be well-equipped. Our armor is the belt of truth, the breastplate of righteousness, the shield of faith, and the helmet of salvation. Our weapons are the Gospel of peace and the sword of the Spirit (Eph. 6:12–14). Our spiritual armor will protect us during battle, while God rebuilds our lives. Our spiritual weapons "have divine power to demolish strongholds" as we move forward in our redeemed life (2 Cor. 10:4). Scriptures tell us there are three ways our armor and weapons are put to use:

WEAPON #1: PRAYER

Jeremiah 29:12–13 implores us, "Then you will call upon me and come and pray to me, and I will listen to you. You will seek me and find me when you seek me with all your heart." God is searching for warriors of prayer. We have been called to active duty on our knees because God knows that to battle through the rubble of our lives we must constantly be connected to Him.

WEAPON #2: SPEAK GOD'S TRUTH

The Word of God is the beacon of hope for all men and women—for others and for ourselves. It is a lamp for our feet and a light for our path (Ps. 119:105). It will guide us during difficult times when the path is hard to see. It will also act as an offensive weapon that will cut through every lie and pretension that the enemy may try to use to discourage, deceive, and distract us. God's plans for family, business, church, government, marriage, and sustained personal victory can be found in His Word. When we live and speak in accordance with it, light and truth are revealed and darkness is dispelled.

WEAPON #3 THE CHURCH

When we stand together as a body of believers, the gates of hell cannot prevail against us (Matt. 16:18). No source of darkness can overcome light—darkness is merely the absence of light. When we stand as one for integrity, honor, truth, and love, darkness will not prevail.

Victory

Nehemiah 6:15–16 tells us that the wall of Jerusalem was rebuilt from the rubble in just fifty-two days. The light of God's glory shined on the Israelites and we're told their enemies became afraid of them and lost their confidence.

It sounds oversimplified, but truth is not complicated: Victory will come when we keep our focus on God because He is our greatest source of confidence in battle. To maintain this confidence and the victory that comes with it, we should march forward on our knees, leaning on the truths of His Word, united with our fellow believers.

God knows us, for we are His (2 Tim. 2:19). He promises us that we can move forward with confidence and rebuild the rubble of our lives, knowing that He has a building plan that He will complete. Take heart. Don't look to the rubble; look to God.

. . . being confident of this, that he
who began a good work in you
will carry it on to completion
until the day of Christ Jesus.

—PHILIPPIANS 1:6

CHAPTER EIGHTEEN

When Bad Things Happen

SEVERAL YEARS AGO I WAS IN WEST PALM BEACH AT THE gravesite of a stillborn baby. I stood with the parents next to the tiny casket, asking God what I could possibly say to comfort this young couple in their time of loss. Words can't reach a pain that deep.

Several years ago a young girl from our church family was playing tennis when she dropped over with a brain aneurysm. We held all-day prayer vigils until the doctors told us that she no longer had any brain activity. Her parents had to make the choice to take her off life support. It ripped my guts out. In anguished confusion, I asked God why He chose this child. She was gone. Can our faith handle these heavy questions and doubts?

I personally believe it's only natural that we ask God why painful things happen in our lives. Most ask, "If God is a loving God; if God is in control; if God is all powerful; if God is all knowing, then why does He allow such injustice? Why does He allow sickness and pain to riddle the bodies of our children? Why does God allow our world to be ripped apart emotionally and relationally? Why does God even allow evil to exist?"

Habakkuk was a man who was distraught at all the violence and injustice happening against God's people. The book that bears his name was written nearly six-hundred years before Christ, but take note of his questions and see if they sound familiar in today's world.

> How long, O LORD, must I call for help, but you do not listen? Or cry out to you, "Violence!" but you do not save? Why do you make me look at injustice? Why do you tolerate wrong? Destruction and violence are before me; there is strife, and conflict abounds. Therefore the law is paralyzed, and justice never prevails. The wicked hem in the righteous, so that justice is perverted. Your eyes are too pure to look on evil; you cannot tolerate wrong. Why then do you tolerate the treacherous? (Hab. 1:2–4, 13*a*)

God's Word teaches us that there will always be mystery in this life. Right now we can only know "in part" (1 Cor. 13:12), but when Jesus returns, we will fully know the mysteries yet uncovered.

Though at times we gain only limited understanding of why things happen the way they do, we need to have confidence that God's ways are always higher than our ways, and His thoughts are greater than our thoughts (Isa. 55:9).

CONSEQUENCE AND GLORY

God established moral and spiritual laws for our benefit. One of those moral laws is free choice. Because we have free choice, we have the right to choose good or evil (Deut. 30:16–20).

Much of the injustice that we see in the world is because someone has chosen to defy the principles of God, which ultimately bears negative consequences. Ezekiel 16:58 says, "You will bear the consequences of your lewdness and your detestable practices,' declares the LORD." Often, these consequences affect more than just the one who chose wrongly, whether the others deserve it or not.

In John chapter nine, the disciples were walking with Jesus when they came across a blind man. Their immediate response was to ask Jesus if the man had sinned or if it was his parents' sin for which the man was now paying the consequences—a kind of generational curse.

Jesus replied that neither the man nor his parents had sinned. He explained that the man was blind so that the glory of God might be revealed through him. Then Jesus walked over to the man and touched him, and his eyes were healed. The disciples saw firsthand that the glory of God was the highest priority.

Sometimes God allows the pain and difficulties of life because He plans to use them as a platform to demonstrate His glory and win back the hearts of men and women. This concept is easy to read in a book but hard to swallow when it's a reality in our lives.

GOD'S TIMETABLE

The Lord begins to answer Habakkuk's second complaint in Habakkuk 2:2: "Then the LORD replied: 'Write down the revelation and make it plain on tablets so that a herald may run with it.'"

We rarely find insight into our circumstances on our timetable, but God promises answers to our questions according to His plan. The revelation Habakkuk was waiting for took more than seventy years to receive. In our microwave age, this would drive us crazy and cause some to curse God. How we react when God takes longer than we think He should says everything about whether or not we believe that God's timing is perfect.

God told Habakkuk that he would not understand His reasoning until the end of the story. Yet, He assures Habakkuk that His motive will not prove false. Though it lingers, though it waits, though it takes more time than you thought necessary, though you cannot understand, though the darkness has come, God says to wait (Hab. 2:3).

Trusting God until the end of the story is the challenge we all face. Fortunately, if we know God, we know that the themes of His stories are always redemption and restoration. These themes will always prevail.

THE RIGHT OUTLOOK

Taking on a different perspective, a heavenly perspective, will help us to endure bad things happening to good people. This doesn't mean we "accept" them as okay, nor does it mean we stop trying to prevent evil and injustice; it just means that when such things occur despite our best efforts to squash them, we defer our lack of knowledge to God's eternal purposes.

We were made for eternity. Though we will have trouble in this life, our hearts confirm that this is not the end of the story (Ecc. 3:11). Some of us will never be able to make sense of what we've gone through in this life, until we face Jesus in eternity.

In response to this knowledge, Paul tells the church in Corinth: "Therefore, we do not lose heart. Though outwardly we are wasting away, yet inwardly we are being renewed day by day" (2 Cor. 4:16). He understood that even though his physical body was deteriorating, his spirit was built for eternity and would get stronger the closer he was to Jesus. What an incredible attitude. With this Paul continues: "For our light and momentary troubles are achieving for us an eternal glory that far outweighs them all" (2 Cor. 4:17).

Paul understood that ultimately there is purpose in pain. It reminds us that what we long for, what we really need, is life without evil, injustice or pain—life as God intended it to be. With this awareness, Paul gained confidence for his life journey—no matter what crossed his path. He kept a heavenly perspective that was determined to see the ultimate hope in the end. "So we fix our eyes, not on what is seen," he says, "but on what is unseen. For what is seen is temporary, but what is unseen is eternal" (2 Cor. 4:18).

To maintain hope and confidence when bad things happen in your life or in the lives of those you love, meditate on the following three characteristics of eternity:

1. *Justice will be revealed.* Second Thessalonians 1:6–7 says, "God is just. He will pay back trouble to those who trouble you and give relief to you who are troubled and to us as well. This will happen when the Lord Jesus is revealed from heaven in blazing fire with his powerful angels." God wants us to release our judgment of others into His hands through forgiveness because He will take care of everything in His way.

2. *We will be healed.* Isaiah writes, "Then your light will break forth like the dawn, and your healing will quickly appear; then your righteousness will go before you, and the glory of the LORD will be your rear guard" (58:8).

3. *We will experience reconciliation.* Romans 5:11 says, "Not only is this so, but we also rejoice in God through our Lord Jesus Christ, through whom we have now received reconciliation." God is going to rebuild the broken things in our lives. When Christ returns, we will see the fullness of His reconciliation.

CULTIVATING A HEART OF ENDURANCE

Our pain will not be wasted. Romans 8:28 says, "And we know that in all things, God works for the good of those who love him, who have been called according to his purpose." Paul doesn't say that all things *are* good; he says that God will work *for the good* in all things, even in the bad things that occur in our lives.

James looks at this news through an optimistic light. He writes, "Consider it pure joy, my brothers, whenever you face trials of many kinds, because you know that the testing of your faith develops perseverance. Perseverance must finish its work so that you may be mature and complete, not lacking anything" (James 1:2–4).

"Therefore," exhorts Paul, ". . . let us fix our eyes on Jesus, the author and perfecter of our faith, who for the joy set before him, endured the cross, scorning its shame, and sat down at the right hand of the throne of God. Consider him, who endured such opposition from sinful men, so that you will not grow weary and lose heart" (Heb. 12:1–3).

In 1965, Admiral Jim Stocksdale became the highest-ranking POW in the Vietnam War. He was in a concentration camp for eight years and was tortured repeatedly. His captors ripped off his fingernails, drove spikes into the most sensitive parts of his body, used electrical shock on him, beat him, and starved him. His experience was horrific.

When Admiral Stocksdale was finally liberated in 1973, he was asked how he managed to never lose confidence. "I never lost faith in the end of the story," he said. "I never doubted not only that I would get out, but also that I would prevail in the end and turn the experience into the defining event of my life, which, in retrospect, I would not trade."[1]

In this life, we might never have a good answer for why bad things happen to good people; this does not mean we should not endure and trust that when the end of the story is revealed, all will make sense.

Don't lose heart in the hard times. Remember that Jesus has been there too. He was sent to this world to endure the same heartaches, pain, and death that we will face so that He would be able to sympathize with our hardships and meet us at our point of need (Heb. 4:15).

Admiral Stocksdale's story should inspire you in dark times. He wouldn't trade those eight years in concentration camp for anything. They were the defining moments in his life in which his character and faith were forged.

Similarly, Habakkuk concluded:

Though the fig tree does not bud and there are no grapes on the vines, though the olive crop fails and the fields produce no food, and though there's no sheep in the pen and no cattle in the stall, yet I will rejoice in the LORD. I will be joyful in God, my Savior. For the Sovereign LORD is my strength; he makes my feet like the feet of a deer, he enables me to go on to the heights. (Hab. 3:17–19)

And He enables us to do the same. Have confidence; the story is not over yet. There is hope because God is finishing our story.

> And we know that in all things
> God works for the good of those
> who love him, who have been
> called according to his purpose.
>
> —ROMANS 8:28

CHAPTER NINETEEN

The Challenge of Grief

A HOT WAVE OF PAIN FLOODED JUDY'S BODY AS SHE HEARD the words no mother wants to hear: "Ma'am, I'm sorry to have to tell you this, but your son is dead." Judy had to force herself through the procedure of the next few hours, talking with her son's friends, neighbors, and the police. Her best friend, trying to help, said, "Judy, you need to go to a church service right away. They are having Christmas Eve services at Christ Fellowship Church."

A few minutes later Judy pulled onto our church property. One of the volunteer parking attendants noticed that she was crying. When Judy mentioned her son's death, he guided her into a convenient parking place and personally escorted her into the building. From there, two women took Judy's arms, led her to a seat, and remained next to her throughout the service, sharing many hugs and tears.

In the midst of the Christmas Eve service, God had a plan for Judy's life and it involved her being there. By the end of the service, Judy understood God's great love for her and received His gift of peace. It was a miracle. That night, one of intense tragedy, became a source of deep, lasting joy. Today, Judy will tell you, "On the night I lost my son, God gave me His."

A TOUCH OF GRIEF

My grandfather's death was my first real encounter with serious grief. He was my mentor—someone I could go to for encouragement and guidance. I miss him more today than ever.

When King David grieved over the death of the son he conceived with Bathsheba, his sorrow was intensified by the realization that the loss was a consequence of his sin. His only consolation was the assurance that God would reunite him with his son in eternity. He said to his servants, "Can I bring him back again? I will go to him, but he will not return to me" (2 Sam. 12:23).

Though the experience of grief is difficult—sometimes unbearable—most of us eventually discover how to move through life. It takes time, and we still carry the memory but somehow we eventually move from hurt back to hope.

There are a lot of factors that determine how we cope with grief—our personality, our support system, and how close we were to the person who died. Typically, people deal with grief in one of two ways: they go into denial to avoid the pain associated with their loss, hoping to forget; or they recognize their grief and seek healing and growth. Dealing with a loss is slow, laborious work. In order for growth to coexist with grief, it is essential to allow oneself to feel all the emotions that arise, as painful as they may be, and to be patient. Regardless of the factors in our situation, we have to reach deep to find confidence and hope to continue living so we don't end up as casualties of grief.

A NORMAL COURSE OF ACTION

Perhaps the most important thing to remember is that mourning is normal and healthy. We should also keep in mind that we are not alone in our grief; others have shared similar losses and can be great outlets for bottled up emotions. Plugging into the comforting encouragement of caring people is a great way to help us through the grief process.

"Carry each other's burdens," Galatians 6:2 urges us, "and in this way you will fulfill the law of Christ." One of the greatest blessings in life is finding someone who will stand by our side in times of pain. One of the greatest privileges is to be that person for someone else.

Some like to say, "If you have faith, you will not experience pain." This is not true. Being a Christian does not mean we get to sidestep the pain of this world—namely, the grief of death. Inevitably, we will have to face disappointment and loss. We will feel pain. It is part of this fallen world. Drawing on God's strength and the strength of others during such times is the best thing available to us. However, expressing sadness is not an insult to God, even when it comes out at unexpected times and places. This is why 1 Peter 5:7 tells us, "Cast all your anxiety on him because he cares for you." It is an invitation to throw our most painful experiences, emotions, and hurts upon our Heavenly Father.

PRINCIPLES OF HANDLING GRIEF

As you work through grief and loss in your life, I suggest that you take the following actions as part of your healing experience. They will help you work through the pain in a healthy and healing manner:

1. *Talk about your loss.* Seek comfort from friends who will listen; let them know you need to talk about what has happened. Good people in your life will try to understand. More importantly, even if they don't know how to respond, they will stand by you as you grieve. They will hold you up when you can't stand on your own. When no words will suffice, the silent support of loving friends is precisely what you need.

2. *Forgive yourself.* Let go of all the things you think you should have said or done. Let them go. Also, forgive yourself for the emotions such as anger, guilt, or embarrassment you may feel while

grieving. God has a handle on all of our emotions, and they are real and often very necessary for our healing. Let Him have them, as ugly or as embarrassing or as awkward as they seem to you now.

3. *Eat well and exercise.* Grief is exhausting, and it can also rob your appetite. To sustain your energy, be sure to maintain a balanced diet and regular exercise. Find a routine that suits you and stick with it. Without physical strength, your efforts to think straight and feel good are often futile.

4. *Treat yourself.* Take naps, read a good book, listen to your favorite music, go to a ball game. Let go of the false notion that it's disrespectful to the memory of the deceased to do something that is fun, distracting, and that you personally find comforting.

5. *Prepare for holidays and anniversaries.* Many people feel especially sad during these times, and the anniversary of the death of a loved one can be especially painful. Make arrangements to be with friends and family members with whom you are comfortable. In fact, plan activities that give you an opportunity to mark the anniversary with something joyful.

Vonette Bright, widow of Bill Bright, told me about the beautiful and meaningful gathering she had with family and friends to celebrate the "first birthday in heaven" of her late husband. Vonette doesn't see the anniversary of Bill's death as a time of mourning. She has the eternal perspective that Bill is rejoicing in his new home with Jesus, so she celebrates it as such.

6. *Share your experience with others who are grieving.* Learning about the grief process through your own experience will help you to support others who have to take that journey too. You may have the opportunity to do this one-on-one, as opportunities arise, or possibly through a grief support ministry in your church.

Remember Judy, the grieving mother who found God's Son during a Christmas Eve service? She has done just this thing. She has

gone through lay counseling training at our church and is now ministering to others experiencing grief.

OUR COMFORT AND STRENGTH

The resurrected and living Christ is our ultimate comforter and
provider during every valley of life. The very fact that He faced
death and overcame it brought with it the benefit of eternal life for
all of us whose lives are His. This is our greatest comfort and our
source of confidence in painful times—that death is but a new and
glorious beginning. When grief happens—and it happens to us all—
we can turn to Christ whose rest and assurance will ultimately
restore our confidence and hope.

Come to me all you who
are weary and burdened,
and I will give you rest.

—MATTHEW 11:28

CHAPTER TWENTY

Investing for Eternity

WHEN DONNA AND I GOT MARRIED, I WAS JUST A SOPHO-more in college on a football scholarship. Housing for married couples was limited so we had to take what was available. Imagine old army huts with paper-thin walls and tiny rooms in which you froze in the winter and fried in the summer; that's where we lived. Our financial situation tightened even more when we found out Donna was pregnant. Money was so scarce that for the first few months of our marriage we lived on peanut butter sandwiches and soup. Needless to say, our married life started out pretty tight.

During those lean times, when the offering plate passed by me, I would sit and struggle internally about what I should give to God. When finances are low it is so easy to think that God should not expect anything from you. But I was raised in a humble home where we believed in honoring God with the first 10 percent of our income. I came to the conclusion that either tithing is a right principle or it isn't; and if it is, we needed to follow it consistently and wholeheartedly. We decided that no matter how little we had, a dime out of every dollar went to God through the local church.

In hindsight, the decision to honor God in our giving was the greatest financial decision I ever made. Since then, I have simply tried to let Him be the Lord of my finances, and He has blessed me beyond measure. Ultimately, I came to understand that if I made it my first priority to invest in eternal things, God would consistently help me meet the needs of my family.

Living day by day with financial confidence has a tremendous effect on how you relate to God and to others. If you are a poor financial manager, it will affect every area of your life. It will hinder you from responding to the will and purpose of God, and it will tarnish your reputation with others. God has given us direction for handling our finances. The counselors at our church deal mostly with the way people handle money or, rather, how money handles people. The subjects of faith and finance are interwoven into the fabric of life, and the Lord wants His people to have all the threads in the right place.

SEEING BEYOND YOURSELF

Perhaps the best financial lesson I've learned is the concept of "seeing beyond myself." Whenever I talk to people about money, this is what I suggest they learn. Philippians 2:4 reinforces this principle: "Each of you should not only look to your own interests, but also to the interests of others."

William Borden is a clear example of this. He was a wealthy Christian who grew up in Chicago as an heir of the Borden milk fortune. During his first year at the prestigious Yale University, Borden committed himself to spending his life as a missionary. From the worldly perspective, it was an unexpected decision for someone with such financial potential.

After graduation, he sailed for Egypt to study Arabic in order to communicate with the Muslims of North India where he believed God had called him. Realizing that his real security was not in his family inheritance, he gave away about a million dollars to various Christian mission organizations.

In his fourth month in Cairo, Borden contracted spinal menin-
gitis and died within weeks. Under the pillow on his deathbed was
found a piece of paper with words that summed up Borden's brief
but dedicated life: "No reserve! No retreat! No regrets!"[1]

His story also poses a personal question to each one of us: Will
we embrace the mission of Christ over our own reserves?

STRETCHING OURSELVES

Investing for eternity requires us to stretch our boundaries. This
is why Paul encouraged the Corinthians, "But just as you excel in
everything—in faith, in speech, in knowledge, in complete earnest-
ness, and in your love for us—see that you also excel in this grace of
giving" (2 Cor. 8:7). Being a good investor in God's eternal enterprise
usually involves stepping out beyond what is comfortable or safe.

A missionary couple who had spent most of their lives in
Central America was about to retire. A local man to whom they
had ministered arrived at their doorstep, having traveled four days
to bring them a departing gift of appreciation: two coconuts.

Although they were genuinely grateful, the couple marveled
aloud that the man would come so far to give them a few coconuts.
The man's response was simple yet profound: "Long walk part of
gift," he said.[2]

Could it be that our mere act of stretching is a gift to the Lord
in and of itself? Is it possible that God is blessed by our willingness
to "go the distance," and travel outside our comfort zone for Him?
Stretching beyond our comforts leads us to the ultimate investment:
sacrifice.

SACRIFICING BOLDLY

When Jesus contrasted the widow's offering in the temple to the
more wealthy givers, He pointed out to His disciples, "They all gave

out of their wealth; but she, out of her poverty, put in everything—all she had to live on" (Mark 12:44). When the widow dropped her two mites into the box, the sound of it rattled in heaven. God takes notice of a heart that is willing to sacrifice even when it hurts.

Author Bryan Chapell tells the story of an incident that took place in his hometown. Two brothers were playing on the sandbanks by the river. One brother ran after the other up a large mound of sand. The mound was not solid, and their weight caused them to sink quickly.

When the boys did not return home for dinner, the family and neighbors organized a search. They found the younger brother unconscious with his head sticking out above the sand. When they cleared the sand to his waist, he awakened.

"Where is your brother?" the searchers asked him. Tears welled up in the young boy's eyes. With a trembling voice, he said, "I'm standing on his shoulders."[3]

The older brother had sacrificed his own life to lift his younger brother to safety.

How bold, how truly sacrificial, is our commitment to God?

A foreign affairs editor for a major news magazine once told the story of the ravaging famine in Somalia, East Africa. In a village decimated by starvation, a photographer noticed a little boy suffering from malnutrition. When the photographer handed a grapefruit to the little boy, he was so weak that he couldn't even handle the grapefruit. A member of the crew cut it in half and gave it to him. He picked it up, looked as if to say thanks, and walked back toward his village. There on the ground was another little boy, the first boy's younger brother, who appeared to be dead, his eyes completely glazed over. His older brother knelt down, bit off a piece of the grapefruit and chewed it for a moment. He then opened up his younger brother's mouth, put the chewed piece in, and worked his brother's jaws up and down.

Later, the news crew learned that the older brother had done that same routine for about two weeks until he himself finally died of malnutrition. The younger brother survived.[4] The story certainly reminds me of what Jesus must have meant when He said there is no greater love than to lay down your life for another (John 15:13). That is bold sacrifice. How much of our lives are we willing to sacrifice for our Lord?

As we begin to apply the principles of investing for eternity, Scripture offers us four benefits:

BENEFIT #1: GOD IS HONORED

Second Corinthians 9:13 says, "Because of the service by which you have proved yourselves, men will praise God for the obedience that accompanies your confession of the gospel of Christ, and for your generosity in sharing with them and with everyone else."

When you give as a faithful steward of what God has given to you, God will be honored and His work will be furthered in the lives of others. We bring glory to God when we are faithful and generous in taking care of others and building His church.

BENEFIT #2: YOUR GIFT IMPACTS OTHERS

Hebrews 13:16 reminds us not to forget to do good and to share with others, "for with such sacrifices God is pleased." Our offerings to God can positively affect others, near and far. Some will have physical and spiritual needs met through our gifts, and others will be inspired by the example of our stewardship to respond with their own contributions.

BENEFIT #3: YOU WILL BE BLESSED

"'Bring the whole tithe into the storehouse,'" says Malachi 3:10, "'that there may be food in my house. Test me in this,' says the LORD Almighty, 'and see if I will not throw open the floodgates of heaven and pour out so much blessing that you will not have room enough for it.'"

When we commit boldly to eternal investment, Scripture promises that our lives will be blessed. We are not told how we will be blessed—financially, emotionally, spiritually, physically, vocationally—we are just told that we *will* be blessed. Some make the mistake of treating the verse like an invitation to strike a deal with God in order to receive a high rate of return for ourselves. In God's economy, we are only blessed in a measure that will bring glory to God. While He enjoys blessing us with financial or vocational or physical abundance, we don't invest in God in order to be blessed right back. Our motive should be one of love and expectation that God's Kingdom will be advanced from our investments.

BENEFIT #4: YOU WILL LAY UP TREASURES IN HEAVEN

"Do not store up for yourselves treasures on earth, where moth and rust destroy, and where thieves break in and steal. But store up for yourselves treasures in heaven, where moth and rust do not destroy, and where thieves do not break in and steal. For where your treasure is, there your heart will be also" (Matt. 6:19–21).

Treasure in heaven is really the bottom line of investing for eternity. Our natural tendency is to expect that our financial commitment to God will get our immediate wants met. That's not what Jesus was telling the people in ancient Galilee. When God becomes the priority in our giving, we will not see the full return until we get to heaven. In fact, if we could see ahead, through heaven's perspective, there would probably be less hesitancy on our part to increase our giving.

The time, talents, and treasures God has given us are most effective when we exercise the confidence to see beyond ourselves, stretch our boundaries, and sacrifice boldly. When we make this kind of growing investment, God will be honored, our gift will impact others, and we will receive multiple blessings. But there is no greater blessing than hearing God comment on how we succeeded in giving to others. "Good work!" He'll say, "You did your job well. From now on, be my partner" (Matt. 25:21, THE MESSAGE). When we invest our resources using God's principles, we will experience confidence in our treasure.

But store up for yourselves treasures
in heaven, where moth and rust
do not destroy, and where thieves
do not break in and steal.

—MATTHEW 6:20

CHAPTER TWENTY-ONE

Pain Doesn't Get Wasted

MY FRIEND DANA WAS STAYING AT A REHABILITATION CENter in Indiantown, Florida. He was dealing with some destructive issues in his life, so I decided to drive out and visit him. As I pulled into the center, I was directed to the barn where Dana was working. When I found him, Dana was standing knee-deep in a pigpen with a large can of feed under his arm. He was covered in mud from the impatient pigs scurrying to be fed. What a scene. Here was this successful businessman, who was usually well dressed, standing in the thick stench of a muddy pen, feeding pigs on a brutally hot day.

As I watched him clomp through the mud, I couldn't help but think about the story of the Prodigal Son. He had squandered his inheritance, only to find himself sleeping in a pigpen, eating with the swine. I was overwhelmed at the thought of the miracle God wanted to do through Dana's life. I got out of the car, walked into the muddy stench, and hugged Dana. I told him I loved him and was proud of his efforts to know God and to work through some of the challenges in his life.

Eventually, Dana got his life turned around and his marriage restored. Today, he runs a ministry where hundreds of people find healing and restoration through the power of Christ. Dana would be the first to tell you that the key to dealing with the pain and abuse of his childhood was getting his life refocused on God. For years, he tried to mask his pain with alcohol and drugs. He was dealing with his hurt in isolation, decreasing his chances of keeping his life intact. The pigpen experience forced his focus off himself. Once he learned how to trust God with his hurt, he gained confidence to take action and rescue the things that mattered most to him.

Another person familiar with hurt is the apostle Paul. He was beaten and left for dead, imprisoned unjustly, stoned, and shipwrecked. He experienced not only physical pain but also the emotional pain of rejection and betrayal. Through his difficulties, Paul learned that God often uses pain to make His plan and purposes clear. Through his writings, Paul shares with us three particular insights on this topic:

INSIGHT #1: PAIN PUTS OUR FOCUS ON GOD

God allows us to experience pain in our lives so that we will turn to Him. In fact, we are never closer to God than when we are hurting. When things are going great, we have a tendency to become self-reliant and overconfident. Subsequently, we can be very casual with God and lose focus on His purpose and mission in our life. When we are in pain, on the other hand, it raises our awareness of how incompetent we are to fix ourselves. Eventually pain takes the focus off us and onto God.

Paul communicated this principle well when he wrote:

To keep me from becoming conceited because of these surpassingly great revelations, there was given me a thorn in my flesh, a messenger of Satan, to torment me. Three times I pleaded with the Lord to take it away from me. But He said to me, "My grace is sufficient for you, for my power is made perfect in weakness." Therefore I will boast all the more gladly about my weaknesses, so that Christ's power may rest on me. That is why, for Christ's sake, I delight in weaknesses, in insults, in hardships, in persecutions, in difficulties. For when I am weak, then I am strong. (2 Cor. 12:7–10)

INSIGHT #2: PAIN GIVES BIRTH TO COMPASSION

Paul quickly learned that his pain could be a vehicle to share God's love. He wrote, "Praise be to the God and Father of our Lord Jesus Christ, the Father of compassion and the God of all comfort, who comforts us in all our troubles, so that we can comfort those in any trouble with the comfort we ourselves have received from God" (2 Cor. 1:3–4).

Pain surrendered to Christ gives us a platform of compassion and mercy. It's harder to sympathize and encourage someone when you haven't experienced the same kind of pain. I believe God allows certain circumstances in our lives so that He can use us to minister to another whose pain might be just as great as or greater than ours.

My friend Lester is a great example of this. He lost his son at two and a half months old. I remember him telling me the pain was so intense that it felt like every hair on his head was aching. In the following days he was desperate and confused, searching for something that would help him survive the tragedy. Lester recalls that despite how horrific the nightmare was, God's comfort came to him in a very real way during his son's memorial service. God strengthened Lester to release his son into His arms.

Though it happened many years ago, Lester has never forgotten the moment God came to him in his loss. I was with him when we visited our friend Harris, who had just lost his son. I watched how Lester was able to comfort Harris the way God comforted him during his own loss. No one could relate to Harris the way Lester did; he had walked the same path of pain before him. With the comfort God had given him, I saw Lester hold Harris in his arms and pray and cry. Lester's comfort strengthened Harris in his most dire time of need.

INSIGHT #3: PAIN HELPS TO REFINE US INTO THE IMAGE OF GOD

God will never waste our pain. He will always use it for good though we may not see it for years, if ever, in this lifetime.

God doesn't want to destroy our lives or to rob us of our peace of mind, but He occasionally allows pain so that we will rely on Him. It is one way He turns around the work of Satan into the work of His righteous kingdom.

When Paul said, "In all things God works for the good" (Rom. 8:28), he didn't say "some" things. God's working for good includes the painful things, the hard things, the difficult things, the things we don't and won't understand, and the things that just don't make sense. It's quite an amazing promise when you fully comprehend what it means. The most pressing question is: Are we willing to receive the promise?

Ultimately, God uses our life circumstances, good or bad, to conform us into the likeness of His Son Jesus. Even through pain, we can grow to be more like Christ.

There are current theologies that teach if you walk with Jesus, you will never have trouble and if you do, you're not praying enough or being righteous enough. I don't see any of this anywhere in the Bible. In fact, Jesus assures us we will have trouble in this world (John 16:33). It is a given. But peace comes from knowing that Jesus has overcome all the pain of the world. In other words, our suffering is not squandered.

The question we should ask when it comes to pain in our lives is not, "Why, God?" but rather, "What, God? What is it you want me to learn?" So often when we are in pain or trouble it seems that we run everywhere except to God. Our first inclination should be to run to God.

When we run to God through prayer and seek His face, we have His permission to ask what His plan is for the situation. He may not tell us right away, but we can still show by our manner that we seek to learn from it, that we seek to use it to grow to be more like Him, and that we trust Him in the midst of it. Don't let your pain go to waste.

PAIN AND POSITIVE OUTCOME

Pain affects us all differently. Some of us run from the pain and attempt to saturate our lives with all kinds of indulgence in order to fill the void. Others become angry and walk away from God's love and the love of families. Still, some of us bury pain somewhere deep inside our souls, allowing it to take root so that bitterness and resentment grow in our hearts. Pain doesn't have to rule our hearts.

God loves us deeply. If we can find a way to trust Him, we will find that His purposes, though mysterious at times, always have our best interest in mind. God can be the great healer, if we let Him. Remember that He loves to come through, to rescue us. In our God, there is healing, peace, and hope, no matter how severe the pain. Run to God in your pain, and He will give you the strength and confidence to press on.

Be merciful and gracious to me, O God,
be merciful and gracious to me, for my soul
takes refuge and finds shelter and confidence
in You; yes, in the shadow of Your wings will I
take refuge and be confident until calamities
and destructive storms are passed.

—PSALM 57:1 (AMPLIFIED)

CONFIDENCE TO OVERCOME

CHAPTER TWENTY-TWO

The Playbook for Confident Living

WHEN I WAS A RUNNING BACK DURING MY HIGH-SCHOOL football days, the plays we used were simple enough that our coach could diagram them on the blackboard. We could easily memorize all of them. When I got into college football, the tables turned. I was shocked when our coaches handed us playbooks as thick as a technical manual for the space shuttle. Though the game remained the same, the level of competition had progressed, and the complexity of the plays reflected that progression.

A playbook outlines plays that are designed to exploit the weaknesses of the opposition and leverage the strengths of the home team, ultimately leading them to victory. Every team uses a playbook, a point of origin by which to navigate the ups and downs of each game. Life reflects many of the same battles and struggles found in sports, especially football. So consequently you would expect it to have some kind of playbook.

The Word of God is our playbook. It provides us with the blueprints needed to succeed in the "down and distance" of life, whether it's first and ten, and we can try something new or fourth and long, and we need a miracle to come through. Like all great playbooks, the

Bible contains deep truths that not only help navigate life's struggles but also can incite complete change and restoration for a person's soul.

Art Williams (president and founder of A. L. Williams and a former football coach), was notorious for making his playbook simple. He focused on the few plays his team performed the best and sought to master them. Yet, even with a simplified playbook, he still had a favorite play; it was the heart of his playbook. Likewise, God's Word is filled with wonderful, applicable truths that can navigate us through various situations. However, there is one passage in Psalms that we can focus on as the heart of God's playbook. Psalm 119 discusses the way the Scriptures speak to us. The final section of this psalm details the three main benefits the Word of God—our playbook—offers us:

BENEFIT #1: GUIDANCE

"May my cry come before you, O LORD; give me understanding according to your word" (Ps. 119:169).

We live in a culture saturated by individualism. It seems like everything, even absolute truth, is up for discussion. It is increasingly difficult to find a point of origin in this mess of cultural relativism. The need for a sound, biblical worldview has never been more important. Without this we are lost.

A person's worldview determines his or her decision-making process. A worldview asks four basic questions:

1. Who am I?
2. Where am I?
3. What is my purpose?
4. What is my eternal destiny?

The Bible offers precious clarity on these issues. Without clarity we become blind guides, hopeless and helpless, searching for answers that end up being as confusing as the questions. The Word of God offers a lucidity that is reflected in all of His created order.

I believe it was Dr. Ken Boa of Reflections ministry who described the universe as having a cosmic architecture—everything from atoms to the expanse of galaxies is woven together with intricate and beautiful symmetry. The artistry of creation points to a Master Artist who intentionally set all of life into motion in order to have a relationship with His masterpiece, us. By understanding our place in God's created order, we are able to answer the worldview questions with confidence:

1. I am God's masterpiece, sought passionately and loved fiercely.
2. I live on a planet in a universe created and sustained by Him.
3. I exist to fulfill His plan for my life, to glorify and enjoy Him.
4. I am destined to an eternity with Him as a result of His saving grace.

However, like all great battles on the field of sports, there is stiff competition. There are many worldviews contrary to the biblical worldview.

Secular humanism bases its playbook on the denial of God and the supernatural. This denial leads the humanist to the conclusion that man is the supreme authority. This worldview dominates secular education and is a kissing cousin with cosmic humanism.

Cosmic humanism is the ultimate religion of self. It is based on cultural relativism—truth is up for grabs, whatever you want to be true, so be it. Both of these worldviews directly oppose the Bible since both defy total and final truth. By exalting self over sacrifice, these worldviews attempt to supplant the biblical worldview.

Around the time that secular humanism began to gain attention, Lew Wallace, a former Civil War general, undertook the assignment of writing a book to discredit the Bible. However, when he plunged into the project, he discovered, to his amazement, that the evidence favored belief in the Bible and its message. This resulted in his conversion to Christ. Instead of writing his originally intended book, Wallace penned the famous novel, *Ben Hur: A Tale of the Christ*, a masterful outcome to Wallace's transformation.[1]

Those who are hungry for the truth and honestly examine the Word of God will embrace the biblical worldview, which guides individuals to the most meaningful way of life.

BENEFIT #2: PROTECTION

"May my supplication come before you; deliver me according to your promise" (Ps. 119:170).

We can develop confidence because of the protection of the Lord in our lives. In this verse, the psalmist is asking God to deliver him from anything that will keep him from reaching the goal line—every possible influence that will mess up his purpose to love God and do His will. The request is for protection from the opponent whose purpose is to keep us from victory.

God's playbook not only encourages us to stand strong, it instructs us how to battle effectively against our enemy and live the most fulfilling life possible. The "Thou shalt nots" in God's Ten Commandments, for example, are not designed to restrict us and keep us from pleasure, but to protect us and provide us freedom to enjoy life at its fullest.

When Donna and I were vacationing in Colorado a few years ago, we decided to take in a local rodeo one evening. I wanted to get into the rodeo spirit, so I dressed up like a cowboy, and instead of sitting in the grandstand where I was supposed to sit, I joined the guys who were sitting on the arena fence. I was having so much fun, being right in the middle of the action . . . until a sixteen-hundred pound Brahma bull tossed its rider and headed straight toward me. Instinctively, I hurled myself to safety as the bull slammed into the fence where I'd been sitting. I was so grateful that fence was there to protect me. But, ultimately, if I had followed directions from the very beginning and sat in the designated areas, I never would've been in harm's way.

The key to enjoying God's protection is to stick with the playbook and follow its instructions. God gave us the Bible to provide clear directions so that we could walk a path that keeps us under His protection and provision, especially in dangerous territory.

BENEFIT #3: STRENGTH

"May your hand be ready to help me, for I have chosen your precepts" (Ps. 119:173).

The final benefit we receive from using God's playbook is the power to transform our lives. The psalmist makes it clear that the strength we need from God's powerful hand is available to us in His written Word. His precepts bring about significant change in the way we live—change, in fact, that we could not bring about on our own.

Peter Deison, in his book *The Priority of Knowing God*, recounts the story of an Indian man named Rahmad who belonged to a gang of burglars. One night they were ransacking a house when Rahmad saw a book with a black cover and thin, gold-edged pages lying on a table. He thought it would be good for rolling cigarettes, so he swiped it. Every night he tore a page out of the book, packed some tobacco in it, and rolled it up for a smoke. One day he noticed that the small words on the page were in his language, so he decided that every evening when he ripped out a page, he would read it before rolling his cigarette. He did this for several weeks until one night something happened. He ripped out the page, read it, but never got around to rolling a cigarette. God spoke to him from the page he was about to smoke. The words cut deep to his core, and Rahmad fell to his knees, crying out for Christ to save him. Much to the astonishment of the authorities, Rahmad walked into the police station and gave himself up. He confessed to all of his crimes and ended up in prison. There in that prison, serving out his time, Rahmad, the former burglar, now a follower of Jesus Christ, led many other men to the Savior.[2]

Rahmad went from smoking the Bible to living the Bible. Now that's quite a transformation. If the Word of God can make such a dramatic change in Rahmad, then it can most definitely change your life as well.

I made the decision several years ago that I would live the rest of my life choosing God's precepts found in the Bible rather than my own preferences, opinions, or even the beliefs of others. I'll be honest with you; there is a lot within the Scriptures I don't understand. However, my confidence in the Bible as the Word of God continually gives me the courage to face more challenges than I can name. It keeps me anchored to my conviction that what I believe is based on the absolute truth. When you continually get a glimpse of what is authentic, frauds are quickly exposed. This is why it is so important to keep the Word of God on our minds and in our hearts.

Confidence gets the upper hand in your life as you faithfully read and apply God's playbook in everyday attitudes and actions. Eventually, you will discover that it lives in you and through you as a guide, a protector, and the source of your strength.

Your word is a lamp to my feet
and a light for my path.

—PSALM 119:105

CHAPTER TWENTY-THREE

Train for Victory

PREPARATION BUILDS CONFIDENCE. WHEN ATHLETES HAVE trained properly and conditioned themselves, they can enter the competition with confidence. The apostle Paul's confidence came from his spiritual training and discipline. In 1 Corinthians 9:24–25 he says, "Do you not know that in a race all the runners run, but only one gets the prize? Run in such a way as to get the prize. Everyone who competes in the games goes into strict training. They do it to get a crown that will not last; but we do it to get a crown that will last forever." As followers of Christ we are challenged to grow spiritually strong and mature so we can be filled with the confidence to win in the contest of life.

In Philippians 3:7–21, Paul gives us these seven principles for our spiritual training. I call these principles the "7-Ups."

PRINCIPLE #1: TOSS UP

Paul experienced true transformation when confronted by God, which caused his reasoning to make a radical turn. He changed the way he viewed life because his mind became renewed in Christ. This is the first of our 7-Ups. Paul *tossed up* all his thinking.

The Word of God says that we are to have the mind of Christ.

In Romans 12:2 we read, "Do not conform any longer to the pattern of this world." Paul is commenting on the patterns of judgment, perspective, and determining values. He is saying, "Learn the difference between conforming and transforming. Undergo a renewing of the mind."

In the original Greek text of the New Testament, the word "renew" means the same as "overhaul," such as overhauling an engine. In other words, our minds need a major overhaul, not just an oil change. There is a certain freedom when we experience a complete overhaul in our thinking. However, freedom attained through God's Word comes with a special revealing factor. It exposes the depth and hideous nature of our pride. We come face to face with the fact that our hearts are rebellious and don't like to submit to a higher authority. A struggle breaks out between the old self and the transformed self. The old self jerks back and says, "I know what I am doing, I don't need to change," while the transformed self says, "Listen to God's Word, it will set you free." The bottom line is that we will never live like Jesus until we start thinking like Jesus. Like Paul, we need to *toss up* our old thinking and let God's Word overhaul our minds.

PRINCIPLE #2: GIVE UP

"For whose [Jesus'] sake I have lost all things" (Phil. 3:8).

We must be willing to *give up* if we expect to move up in our relationship with Christ. We need to say, "I'm turning loose the things that need to go. I'm going to reprioritize my life." This is the second of the 7-Ups: *Give up*.

We tend to put things into nice neat boxes on our priority shelves. We like to list out our priorities: God, family, job, clubs, etc. These are all good things, right? The disparity we want to look at here is the difference between the *good things* and the *best things*.

Being part of the Lions Club isn't necessarily a bad thing, but does it get in the way of the best thing that God has for you?

Our culture likes to clutter itself with busyness. Most of us run to and fro, doing things that are good, but in the helter-skelter pace of life we often buzz right by that one gleaming gem that God had for us. It is time to trim the fat from our lives and focus on doing the things that really matter, the thing whispering in your ear right now as you read this, such as: *Yes, go ahead on that mission trip; I will provide the funds.* God is whispering to you, asking you to cast off the things that are holding you back from seeing the fulfillment of His plan in your life.

Hebrews 12:1 makes the case in point, ". . . let us throw off everything that hinders us and the sin that so easily entangles, and let us run with perseverance the race that is marked out for us." Anyone can run a sprint. But life is not a sprint. The race to real fulfillment through Christ is a marathon. Have you ever seen a marathon runner wearing a backpack? Of course not. If you are going to run a 10K or 20K course, you strip down to the basics. You don't even carry a water bottle. You get your nourishment along the way from people cheering you on, handing you cups of Gatorade, and splashing water at you. Like the distance runner, we need to start traveling lighter in life. We need to *give up* the junk—even some of the good stuff—so we can keep moving toward and receiving God's best.

PRINCIPLE #3: BUILD UP

Learning to *build up* is the third of the 7-Ups. Paul says in Philippians 3:12, "Not that I have already attained all this or have already been made perfect, but I press on to take hold of that for which Jesus Christ took hold of me."

"Press on." These words imply a continuance, a process of building upon the victories and obstacles that leads toward a goal. Paul was yanked from his former purpose of persecuting Christians, to his new destiny, which was to proclaim the good news of Christ. Paul's life emulated a marathon runner; building speed, building endurance, and building confidence in order to, one day, seize the prize. God grabbed hold of Paul and Paul's response in this verse tells us, "I'm grabbing hold of God. I'm getting a good grip here. There is a purpose and destiny with my name on it, and I'm going to hang on to it by faith with all my heart."

We, too, must get a grip. We need to hold on as tight as we can to our life's purpose and destiny by faith in Jesus Christ, and build up that marathon faith through obedience to Him. In Philippians 3:16, Paul emphasizes that we must "live up to what we have already attained." In other words, we have more than enough of God's revealed Word. The question is: What do we do with what we already know? Living out the truth we possess, moment by moment, in obedience to God, is the way to make spiritual progress with freedom in Christ.

PRINCIPLE #4: PRESS UP

"Brothers, I do not consider myself yet to have taken hold of it. But one thing I do: Forgetting what is behind and straining toward what is ahead, I press on toward the goal to win the prize in which God has called me heavenward in Christ Jesus" (Phil. 3:13–14).

How often do you see someone in a race look back? Not very often. Whenever a sprinter gets into the blocks, he is focused on something in the distance ahead of them: the finish line. As soon as the gun sounds, everything in his mind and body is focused forward; there is complete commitment—no turning back. How does this principle relate to life issues? So often we are overcome by a sense of guilt and shame by our pasts. At times it is paralyzing. We keep looking back and it keeps us from moving forward.

Paul knew what he was writing about. He had issues that could've easily haunted him in his sleep. Imagine Paul tossing and turning in cold sweats in the middle of the night, hearing the cries of those he had persecuted and killed. The accuser, Satan, could dig up those haunting memories and use them to torment him. But Paul turned the shadows of his former life over to his forgiving God and focused on "straining . . . press[ing] on toward the goal to win the prize."

Like Paul, we are called to *press up* and put the past in the hands of the Redeemer. Jesus left us with the Counselor, His Holy Spirit, to minister to us and to strengthen our minds and hearts. When the lies of Satan seek to bring you down into the depths of shame, remember that we live in victory. Press on; press up further now, until the end.

PRINCIPLE #5: TEAM UP

"Join with others in following my example" (Phil. 3:17).

Teaming up with others is a must in your journey of spiritual growth. God never intended for you to fly solo. Followers of Christ are to be united, and it takes a team effort to make that happen. We need each other. Proverbs 27:17 puts it this way, "As iron sharpens iron, so one man sharpens another." Instead of putting each other on edge, we are to edge each other on by encouraging, protecting, inspiring, and lovingly holding each other accountable.

When I was a high-school football coach several years ago, our Palm Beach Gardens High School team played the Ft. Pierce Central state champion team. Both teams were 5 and 0, undefeated. We played them at their homecoming game and, I am proud to say, we let them have it, winning by a walloping 39 to 6. At the end of every game, our team would huddle together in the center of the field.

During this particular game, the video camera caught our punter Kerry wandering off from the huddle, waving his helmet around, doing his own celebrating. The camera pointed away from Kerry just as two

Central players blindsided him. When the camera panned back to Kerry, he was lying on the turf, knocked cold. He should have stayed inside the huddle. So should you and I. We never know who or what might come up behind us and knock us flat. Always make sure you *team up*.

PRINCIPLE #6: POWER UP

If we think we can live the Christian life by our own brains and brawn, we are an accident waiting to happen. We need the daily filling of the Holy Spirit to sustain us in life's marathon.

Corrie ten Boom once noted that trying to do the Lord's work in your own strength is the most confusing, exhausting, and tedious of all work; but, when you are filled with the Holy Spirit, the ministry of Jesus just flows out.[1] Make certain you take every opportunity to *power up*.

PRINCIPLE #7: FINISH UP

God has called us to be strong finishers in this marathon of spiritual growth. In Philippians 3, Paul had his mind on heaven. He said that our lowly bodies would become like our Lord's glorious body (vs. 21). It is easy to forget the finish line in the midst of the daily grind. We can have so much else on our minds—so much else to worry about and to accomplish. But Paul reminds us that a day is coming when the only thing that is going to matter to us is hearing the words, "Well done, good and faithful servant!" (Matt. 25:21).

Henry Ford was asked how to be successful. His answer was "If you start something, finish it."[2] That is true for us on our spiritual journey. The key is that we need to be determined to run the race through to the finish line. So gang, let's be up for God's 7-Ups; let's train ourselves spiritually to discover greater confidence in life each day and *finish up* strong.

Brothers, I do not consider myself
yet to have taken hold of it.
But one thing I do:
Forgetting what is behind and
straining toward what is ahead,
I press on toward the goal
to win the prize for which
God has called me
heavenward in Christ Jesus.

—PHILIPPIANS 3:13–14

CHAPTER TWENTY-FOUR

The Dangers of Compromise

ONE DAY A HUNTER IN THE WOODS CAME UPON AN ENOR-
mous bear. As the hunter raised his rifle to shoot the great big griz-
zly bear, the bear called out, "Can't we talk this over like two sober,
intelligent beings?"

The hunter lowered his gun and said, "What's to talk over?"

"Well, for instance" said the bear, coming closer, "what do you
want to shoot me for?"

"Simple," grunted the hunter, "I want a fur coat."

"Well, all I want is a good breakfast," said the bear. "I'm sure we
can sit down and sensibly work this out." So they sat down to work
out an agreement. After a while, the bear got up all alone. They had
reached a compromise. the bear had his breakfast, and the hunter
now had on his fur coat.[1]

A STORY OF COMPROMISE

Be careful that you are not eaten alive by compromise. Samson
is a prime example of one who constantly struggled with the issue of
compromise. His story is found in the book of Judges, chapters
13–16. Samson was called by God to live according to the Nazarite
vow because God chose to use him to deliver the Israelites from the
Philistines.

Three things marked the Nazarite vow:

1. Nazarites were never to touch or eat anything that God deemed as unclean. This abstinence was a symbol of purity before God.
2. Nazarites never drank wine or fermented beverages. They were always careful to guard against the appearance of drunkenness or losing soundness of mind.
3. Nazarites never put a razor to their hair. Hair was representative of God's covering on their life. It was sacred, never to be touched or taken for granted.

The Nazarite vow demonstrated a man's covenant of commitment and honor to God. Samson understood and respected this covenant . . . until he met Delilah, a beautiful temptress that the Philistines used to discover the secret to Samson's great strength.

In his pride, Samson thought he was strong enough to resist Delilah's seductive nature. When Delilah first asked what the secret to his strength was, he told her that if he was bound with young willow branches, he would become as weak as any normal man. Soon after, Samson fell asleep and Delilah tied him up in willow branches. She then shouted, "Arise, Samson, the Philistines are upon you!" Samson jumped up and saw that he was bound. He tore the willow branches loose and fought off the Philistines.

It might seem that Samson should be aware of the deceptive motives of his companion. Unfortunately, he was blinded to her tactics. Twice more Samson played her little game, each time lying about the secret to his strength. Finally, Delilah became infuriated and pleaded with Samson for the truth. She manipulated Samson, claiming that he didn't love her if he wouldn't confide in her. Her persistence and nagging paid off; in a moment of indiscretion and vulnerability,

Samson told Delilah everything. He confided in her about his Nazarite vow, explaining that if his hair was cut, his strength from God would leave him; he would be as weak as any other man.

Delilah sent word back to the rulers of the Philistines and after Samson fell asleep, she called one of the men to shave the seven braids of hair on Samson's head. Then she called Samson as she had three times before, "The Philistines are upon you!"

Samson woke from his sleep, powerless and unaware that the Lord had left him (Judges 16:20). His strength was gone, along with the blessing of God, because he broke his covenant.

While this event is what ultimately broke Samson's covenant with God, his demise didn't start there. It was a downward spiraling lifestyle of compromise that finally led him away from the source of his strength and protection.

One such compromise occurred when Samson ate honey from the carcass of a lion he killed just days earlier. He chose his hunger over keeping his vow of abstinence from unclean foods. Samson was also a regular attendee at parties and banquets where he consumed wine. His thirst for pleasure often outweighed the discipline of his covenant. Eventually, Samson made the ultimate compromise by giving away the secret to his strength. The mistake left him blinded and shackled, working a grindstone that was meant for an animal. His story stands out as a stark example of the effects of sin. The blinding, binding, and grinding nature of sin was vividly evident in Samson's life.

THE DELILAH SPIRIT

Like an army waiting for its enemy to compromise its position, our enemy seeks to manipulate and compromise our faith. When we live in a covenant relationship with God and walk in purity and sound judgment, we allow Him to be the covering in our lives. He becomes our strength, and ultimately, we discover His purpose, mission, and destiny for us. Still, we must always be ready for the "Delilah spirit" to rear its head. The Delilah spirit prowls, seeking to rob us of our identity in Christ through subtle compromises. It eventually leads us to break covenant with God.

Everything in our culture is trying to lure us away, giving us the impression that we are strong enough and wise enough in and of ourselves. If we take this bait and venture out on our own, it usually doesn't take long before we find out just how powerless we really are. When we step out from under God's covering, like Samson, we become vulnerable to the enemy's attack, his plan of subtle compromise to God's will. It is vital that we avoid compromises, even small ones. To do so, we can't let anything lure us away from our relationship to God.

RESTORATION THROUGH MERCY

"But the hair on his head began to grow again after it had been shaved" (Judges 16:22).

This verse brings hope to Samson's story. The regrowth of Samson's hair is symbolic of the mercy of God. Even though he broke his covenant, God still remained faithful to Samson. As the hair on his head began to grow again, I trust that Samson reached up and felt it and became fully aware that God's mercy was still available to him. He cried out to God, asking Him for another chance to bring glory to Him. And God gave him the opportunity.

The Philistines planned to make a spectacle of Samson in the temple of their false gods. As he was led out, Samson asked to be put near the biggest support pillars so he could lean against them. While they strapped him against the pillars, Samson cried out to God for strength. The power of God came upon him again like it had been before, and with a great force, Samson pushed over the pillars and the temple crumbled to the ground, taking his life and the lives of many Philistines who were enemies of God's people. Through this final display of strength, God was glorified. Samson had been redeemed.

Samson's story gives me a lot of hope that God will show us mercy no matter where we are in life, whether we have compromised here and there or totally broken covenant. God's mercy is always available, ready to forgive, redeem, and restore us to our home.

I don't know where you are with God, but I do know that if we desire the confidence that His strength and covering provide, we need to be people who deeply respect His requests and commands. We should always be aware of the dangers waiting on the other side of compromise—the blinding, binding, grinding effects of sin. Yet even if we've given in, we can still be free of those consequences and be restored back to covenant with God once again.

Chuck Colson was a bright young attorney in a place of influence on the White House staff. Blinded by the glare of power, he engaged in a series of choices that were outside the limits of the law. Colson and other members of the Nixon staff thought they could get away with it, that their status would protect them. However, the Watergate scandal was uncovered and several went to prison, including Chuck Colson.

Colson was so deceived by power's lure that he became bound by it and eventually gave in to compromise. Sitting in that dismal prison cell with his reputation destroyed, his career over, his power and influence gone, Colson had nowhere to turn but to God. Colson found Christ and soon began to see God's merciful redemption of his life. He resolved to serve God when he got out of prison and help others to discover Christ's mercy. Today, he leads a prison ministry and is one of the most highly respected Christian leaders of our day.[2]

Colson's story is a modern-day reminder that compromise still robs us of God's purpose, blessing, and strength. It also reminds us that God is as merciful today as He was several thousand years ago during Samson's day. He can redeem and use any broken life as long as it remains under the covering of His guidance. This should give us great confidence, no matter how many compromises we've made. We can still bring glory to God. Be on guard against anything that would compromise your faith and commitment. Compromise always erodes our confidence in life.

Be self-controlled and alert . . .

—1 PETER 5:8

CHAPTER TWENTY-FIVE

We All Need a GPS

ONE DAY I WAS DEEP-SEA FISHING WITH A FRIEND AND noticed his boat had a Global Positioning System on board. My friend likes to travel to the Bahamas once in a while, and this system helps him navigate to his desired location. With the GPS, he has confidence to guide his boat through rough and calm seas. But for the navigation system to work properly, it needs to be calibrated on a regular basis. One small glitch can send him way off course.

This is what happened to Korean Airlines Flight 007. In September of 1983, the airliner took off from Anchorage, Alaska bound for Seoul, Korea. Five and a half hours into the flight, a Soviet fighter plane shot Flight 007 down. The incident immediately stirred international outrage during a politically unstable time. Why would the Soviet fighter take out an unarmed commercial jet? Years later, it was discovered that the Korean plane's guidance system had been off by two degrees. This led the flight hundreds of miles off course and, eventually, into restricted air space. Tragically, this small, seemingly insignificant detail was responsible for a tragedy that took 296 innocent lives.[1]

SPIRITUAL NAVIGATION

God gave us an internal GPS—the Holy Spirit—designed to guide us through the highs and lows of life and keep us from perilous situations. We all need this GPS to not only help us understand our current location but also to determine what course we should follow. When we set our course with the wrong coordinates, we could spiritually and physically end up in a dangerous situation.

When I was in high school, my friends and I loved to hang out at a local restaurant called Carter's. All the kids drove around in their cool cars. I drove around in an old '48 Plymouth that my parents gave me. It wasn't cool even in 1948. I typically hid it in the alley and leaned against sharp-looking cars as our friends drove by.

One night at Carter's is forever burned into my memory. Some friends of mine pulled up in their '56 Chevy. Now, *that* was a cool car. They asked me to go cruising with them, and initially I agreed. As they opened the car door for me to get in, I saw my friend Benny who lived down the street from me, and then noticed that all the guys had a bottle of beer in their hands.

I stopped. Even though everything in me wanted to be seen in that cool car with my friends, I just knew I couldn't. I backed up and declined their offer. They laughed and egged me on, but I wouldn't do it.

Later that night as I was driving home from Carter's in my old Plymouth, I saw a burst of light around the corner on the highway. A car had hit an embankment and burst into flames. As my car approached the wreck, I saw that it was the '56 Chevy. Terror gripped me as I thought about my friends fighting for their lives in that fire. Two of the boys in the front seat were thrown from the wreckage and were seriously injured. I then frantically began to search for Benny. I found him lying in a ditch. My heart sank. He had been thrown through the back window when the car hit the embankment. He was pronounced dead on the scene. Later that night, when I was at home washing the blood from my hands after lifting my friend from that ditch, I suddenly remembered how close I had been to being in that ditch with him.

Why didn't I get into the car? I wanted so much to hang out with my friends and go cruising, but something in me sent up a red flag. I believe my decision was ultimately based on a God-given guidance system. I had a relationship with God back then, even at a young age, and I believe it served as a discerning filter. Alarms went off in me, and while I couldn't explain it, I knew I was not to get in that car. The Holy Spirit not only warned me, He protected my life that night.

SPIRITUAL BREATHING

Listening to the Holy Spirit will allow us to sidestep spiritually compromising circumstances. John 16:13 says, "But when He, the Spirit of truth, comes, He will *guide* you into all the truth; for He will not speak on His own initiative, but whatever He hears, He will speak; *and He will disclose to you what is to come*" (NASB, emphasis mine). Jesus left us with the Holy Spirit to act as our internal guidance system keeping us from spiritual danger. It is critical that we maintain close fellowship with Him—that we regularly fine-tune our GPS—in order to receive clear direction.

To prepare ourselves for divine guidance we must "be filled with the Spirit" (Eph. 5:18 NASB). This statement is an imperative rather than an option for those who desire to remain on God's perfect path. How are we to activate the filling of the Holy Spirit in our lives? Dr. Bill Bright clearly illustrated this process. He said we are to engage in a type of "spiritual breathing." First, we *ex*hale by confessing to God all of the attitudes and actions in our experience that put self in the driver's seat and send Him to the back seat. Then, we *in*hale by praying to invite the Holy Spirit to take control of our thought life and our behavior.[2]

Bob Mumford's book, *Take Another Look at Guidance*, compares determining confidence in God's guidance with a sea captain's docking procedure:

> A certain harbor in Italy can be reached only by sailing up a narrow channel between dangerous rocks and shoals. Over the years, many ships have been wrecked, as navigation is hazardous. To guide the ships safely into port, three lights have been mounted on three huge poles in the harbor. When the three lights are perfectly lined up and appear as one, the ship can safely proceed up the narrow channel. If the pilot sees two or three lights, he knows he's off course and in danger.[3]

Similarly, God provides us with four beacons to guide us, and the same rules of navigation apply. When the messages we receive from these four sources are aligned, we can have assurance of God's clear path.

BEACON #1: GOD'S WORD

God's Word provides us with the clearest direction. That is why it is paramount to spend time reading, memorizing, and meditating over Scripture. We so often see this discipline as "something we should do" to be good followers of Christ but fail to recognize the critical value it has to our direction in life. The psalmist writes, "I have hidden your word in my heart that I might not sin against you" (Ps. 119:11). Sin is missing the mark. The power of the Bible guides us so we won't miss the mark God has for us. If we are to discern the Holy Spirit's guidance, it is imperative to get to know God's voice through His Word.

BEACON #2: PRAYER

Prayer is the battery of our GPS. Authentic prayer includes two-way communication. Not only do we need to give praise, be thankful, and confess when we pray, but we also need to listen to what God wants to say to us. Hearing His voice takes discipline and a good bit of silence. Observing times of silence will strengthen our prayer time as we allow the buzz of culture to die down and the still voice of God to speak freely to our hearts. Here are some further suggestions to enhance your prayer life:

- Take a prayer walk in a quiet place. During the walk, ask God to speak to you specifically about a certain situation or in general about your current circumstances.
- Worship God through reflection. Listen to praise music and reflect on the words. Offer thanksgiving for how God specifically provides for you.
- Make your requests known to God. As you reflect on God's value in your life, invariably your perspective will change. Problems become manageable because God gains supremacy in your life. Allow Him to speak peace to your problems.

BEACON #3: CIRCUMSTANCES

Our circumstances, when properly interpreted, can be a vital part of God's guidance. There are two types of circumstances that God uses to lead us: closed doors and open doors. Some Christians think that a closed door is Satan's attempt to prevent God's plan from happening in their lives. Others believe the closed door is God's way of saying no to that pursuit.

Spiritual discernment allows us to discover God's purpose in the open and closed doors of life. You can often interpret the circumstances of life by determining:

- If the unfolding situation is a test from the Lord that you need to endure
- If you are reaping the consequences of a sin from which you should repent
- If it is an attack by the enemy that should be resisted
- If it is persecution that should be endured with God's grace

It is important to note that circumstances only imply possibilities. For example, receiving a scholarship would suggest the possibility of attending a particular college, but this circumstance should align properly with the other guidance factors in order for it to be the right decision. Compare all circumstances with the Word of God and take them before God in prayer. When peace comes—a consistent sense of assurance that this is within God's will—we can step out in confidence.

BEACON #4: CHURCH FELLOWSHIP

There is no substitute for fellowshipping with other believers. Fellowship is dynamic because it affects the way we think and act toward God and each other. We encourage people to get involved in small groups in our church because it cultivates a community of believers who care, encourage, and exhort one another on a regular basis. God will often reinforce His guidance for our lives through others who love us and Him.

LIGHTS IN THE HARBOR

Relationships take work and commitment to be fruitful. Our relationship to God is no different. Like the lights in the harbor, we must incorporate these methods in harmony with each other in order to move forward in intimacy with Christ. As we do this, we gain confidence in our decision making by trusting in God's Word, communicating with Him through prayer, accurately discerning our circumstances, and loving "the brotherhood of believers" (1 Peter 2:17). Our faith grows as our relationship with God deepens. With more effectiveness than any fancy satellite-oriented navigation system, we gain the confidence to make right decisions and take right actions that will shape our lives for the good.

> But when he, the Spirit of truth, comes,
> he will guide you into all truth.
>
> —JOHN 16:13

CHAPTER TWENTY-SIX

Driven by a Dream

ALL OF US ARE DRIVEN BY SOMETHING. WHETHER IT IS A job or money or a relationship, the list is large. Many are even driven by their fears and doubts. I believe that God wants us to be driven by His dreams for us. "'For I know the plans I have for you,'" declares the Lord, "'plans to prosper you and not to harm you, plans to give you a hope and a future'" (Jer. 29:11). God designed us for a distinct purpose, a dream that we will see unfold if we learn to put our confidence in His timing and tactics. This is sometimes difficult.

Joseph was a man driven by a God-given dream that took him down paths that seemed to lead him away from everything good. Yet he remained confident in God's ability to carry out His purpose.

Joseph's dream offended his brothers who were insulted and outraged to hear their brother predict that they would one day bow before him as his servants. This detail of the dream seemed to cause Joseph more harm than good—inciting his resentful brothers to sell him to a slave caravan headed for Egypt. Joseph may have been considered dead to his family, but not to God. He still had a plan, and it was only beginning to unfold.

When Joseph's integrity and wisdom distinguished him from the other servants in Potiphar's household, Joseph no doubt thought the dream was about to come true—until he was cruelly betrayed by his master's wife and thrown into prison. But even then, God's plan was still at work. Joseph found favor with the warden and was eventually given charge of the entire prison. There he encountered two servants of Pharaoh who were impressed with Joseph's gift to interpret their dreams. Joseph asked the king's butler, "Would you please remember me, and tell the king I am in this prison unjustly?" But this path, too, seemed like a dead end when the servant forgot all about Joseph once he was allowed to return to the palace. But God's timing hadn't come yet (Gen. 40).

Years later, the king had a nightmare that neither he nor his wise men could interpret. Then the butler remembered his promise. The king was so impressed with Joseph's interpretation of the dream and his wisdom that he appointed *him* as the man in charge during the seven years of abundance and the seven years of famine (Genesis 41).

When Joseph's family depleted their supply of food and could no longer grow crops during the famine, they were forced to humble themselves and travel to Egypt for help. They entered the city, approached the man who could help them, and bowed before him to plead their case (Gen. 42). They didn't know it was their "dead" brother before whom they bowed, but God knew all along this was how it would be (Gen 45:1–8).

The story of Joseph reminds us that God will often use unpredictable—even unenviable—means to accomplish His purposes. Joseph was a young man who had been thrown into a pit, sold into slavery, and confined to prison—all to end up as the king's right-hand man. It was not a pretty path, but it was the best path. Through Joseph, God sustained His people, the Israelites, during the time of the famine. In order to do this, God used the very thing that seemed to ruin Joseph's life to glorify Himself, redeem His people, and honor His servant Joseph who trusted Him all the way.

When we step back and look at the unexpected life of Joseph, we find three secrets that can help us remain confident in God's plan for our own lives:

SECRET #1: NEVER LET CIRCUMSTANCES CONTROL YOUR ATTITUDE

I recently heard a story about a little boy in the dugout during a Little League game. A stranger came up to him and asked, "Son, what's the score?"

"Fourteen to nothing," the little boy replied, his gaze still fixed on the game.

The man looked shocked. "You mean, you are losing fourteen to nothing?" The boy nodded. "Well, aren't you discouraged, young man?"

"No," the boy replied. "We haven't even been up to bat yet."[1]

Joseph had to labor for years in slavery and injustice but, as far as we know, his attitude never wavered. He trusted the God-given dream he had received, and as a result, he saw God's blessing in the end.

Many a great leader have grasped the vital importance of maintaining a positive attitude in every circumstance:

- D. L. Moody: "I am not the only one, but I am only one. I cannot do everything, but I can do something, and that which I can do by the grace of God, I will do."[2]
- John Maxwell: "I once read in the Cox Report on American business that 94 percent of all Forbes 500 executives attribute success more to attitude than to any other ingredient."[3]
- Peter Lowe: "The most common trait I've found in all successful people is that they have conquered the temptation to give up."[4]
- Earl Nightingale: "We become what we think about."[5]

- Viktor Frankl: "Everything can be taken away from a man but one thing, to choose one's attitude in any given set of circumstances, to choose one's way."[6]

Sometimes life's score doesn't look very promising—like Joseph or the Little Leaguer, we might be down by a lot of runs—but a positive attitude can give us the confidence to step up and take our best swing. If the game's not over, God can still come through.

SECRET #2: ALWAYS FIND WAYS TO ADD VALUE

Joseph always managed to positively impact the people around him, whether a slave, a servant, a prisoner, or the king's righthand man. I imagine he always considered what God would have him say or do in every situation he faced. He never doubted that God could use him.

Like Joseph, these men understood that the more value you add, the more value you receive:

- George Washington Carver: "No individual has any right to come into the world and go out of it without leaving behind him distinct and legitimate reasons for having passed through it."[7]
- Dr. Martin Luther King, Jr.: "Life's most persistent and urgent question is: 'What are you doing for others?' It has been said that you can not hold a torch to light another man's path without it brightening your own."[8]

We add value when we look for the best in others and help to bring out the best in them. Learn to speak affirmation to others and look for ways to help.

John Maxwell always infuses the question, "How can I help you today?" into our conversations. John is always looking to add value. Remember, as you add value to others, value will be added to you.

SECRET #3: LIVE WITH INTEGRITY

In 1912, fifteen hundred people lost their lives when the Titanic went down. Only six small slits below the water line compromised the hull of that great ship.[9] Similarly, it's often the small things in our own lives that cause us to lose our integrity. We have to guard against even the smallest missteps. When we do this, we can be certain that our lives will always carry with them great impact on the lives of others.

Joseph's life is a good example. Joseph would not compromise his faith or the standard he set for himself. His consistency and faith were noticed by the powerful people around him, those who did not honor or believe in the one true living God of Abraham, Isaac, and Jacob. Joseph was trustworthy, and people of high position knew they could put him in charge. Potiphar, the prison warden, and Pharaoh all attested to Joseph's reliability.

To maintain integrity is to never compromise. When Potiphar's wife tempted Joseph, he said to her, "No one is greater in this house than I am. My master has withheld nothing from me except you, because you are his wife. How then could I do such a wicked thing and sin against God?" (Gen. 39:9). Joseph's statement speaks perfectly of his heart toward God and his respect for the position in which God had placed him. He trusted that God knew best and that He was guiding him in the smallest details even when appearances suggested otherwise. This is why he ultimately saw his dream fulfilled.

Abolitionist Elijah Lovejoy believed this to the end. The Presbyterian minister's heart was broken over the slavery in our nation, and he fearlessly preached against it from the pulpit. Lovejoy also opened a printing press, where he sent out fliers on the abolishment of slavery. There were many who violently opposed and threatened him.

Eventually, the opposition came to a tragic head: An angry mob burned down his printing press and then hanged him. Many would have said Elijah's life was a forgotten waste—just more collateral damage from a tragic era. However, one young man read many of Elijah Lovejoy's articles and was inspired to action. The man was Abraham Lincoln.[10]

HOLD YOURSELF TO A HIGHER STANDARD

The astonishing detail about the life of Joseph is that he never compromised in the face of rejection, temptation, or hardship. He had every reason to cave in or give up—even take advantage of certain situations for his own gain—but through it all he kept his faith, lived with honor, and is remembered for his amazing perseverance and integrity.

Joseph's life offers a high standard for us to uphold; however, God's constant provision, timely strength, and rich blessing make the standard worth upholding. In the end, a key message of the life of this servant of God is that when we trust God to lead our steps and then follow in them no matter what, our paths may not always be smooth. However, we can be certain that God's path for us will never take us out of reach of God's provision, protection, and blessing. When we rely on the God who is for us, no enemy can defeat us. With firm commitment to pursue God's purpose for our lives, we can live with confidence that His dream, our dream, will come true.

Therefore, my dear friends, as
you have always obeyed—not only
in my presence, but now much more
in my absence—continue to work out
your salvation with fear and trembling.

—Philippians 2:12

CONFIDENCE IN TOMORROW

CHAPTER TWENTY-SEVEN

Hidden Treasure

WHEN I WAS YOUNG, I WAS MORE THAN A KID . . . I WAS AN action hero. I loved to play all my favorite characters. Davy Crockett lived again through me. I searched for buried treasure with Captain Kidd. Every day was an adventure waiting to be discovered.

Mention the words "hidden treasure" to adults and heads will still turn. Many researchers and historians claim that in Florida, where I live, there are more buried treasures than in any other state. They say there is $165 million worth of sunken treasure still waiting to be found. If you have the persistence and equipment to search for it, you might stumble on a fortune.

Discovering hidden gold and jewels is fascinating though most of us will never get near a sunken Spanish galleon or a pirates' secret cave. Yet, there is a treasure within our reach. There is something within us all that brims with adventure, anticipation, and great wealth.

PERSONAL TREASURE

People spend millions of dollars every year trying to discover who they really are when the real discovery is "Christ in you, the hope of glory" (Col. 1:27). But in order to discover this personal treasure, we must cultivate an intimate relationship with our Savior.

Christ cultivates a degree of confidence that empowers us with a supernatural advantage for life. Most people would give anything for true strength and enduring satisfaction, but they fail to realize that it cannot be accomplished by human effort alone. This is why Paul told the Roman believers "we are more than conquerors" *in Christ* (Rom. 8:37). Later, to the church at Philippi, he asserted "I can do all things *through Christ* who strengthens me" (Phil. 4:13 NKJV, emphasis mine).

When Helen Keller lost her sight and hearing as a child, at a time when medical technology was not advanced, the possibility for a meaningful life seemed nonexistent. However, through the dedicated tutoring of Anne Sullivan, Helen came to realize value and strength do not come from leveraging external abilities. Her writing and speaking gained her great fame as she turned her blindness and deafness into an advantage and inspired many to overcome their physical disadvantages. She is a great example of what it means to tap into the treasure within us.[1]

FELLOWSHIP TREASURE

A second treasure within our reach can be found in our relationships with others. Just as buried treasure must be unearthed, we must crack the superficial surface of relationships to encounter the wealth of meaningful fellowship.

Genuine friendship gives encouragement, recognizes value, bestows honor, and demonstrates acceptance. There is a reciprocity that occurs in true fellowship: when we validate the value of others they will, in turn, value us.

Anne Sullivan, Helen's God-sent teacher, is a good example of this. Anne's own dramatic journey from hopelessness to success is a story in itself. She also had to overcome a childhood of partial blindness, rejection, and rebellion. She shared this inner treasure when she mentored Helen Keller. Without Anne Sullivan, Helen might never have found the treasure within her. Yet together they doubled the value of their treasure. It's wise to always look at others fully confident that there is hidden treasure waiting to be discovered within them.

THE BIBLICAL TREASURE

The Word of God overflows with boundless jewels. It reveals the majesty and wonder of God, enabling us to know Him better. If only we will search it out, it is full of mystery and adventure waiting to be discovered. This is why Paul wrote to the young pastor Timothy:

> From infancy you have known the holy Scriptures, which are able to make you wise for salvation through faith in Christ Jesus. All Scripture is God-breathed and is useful for teaching, rebuking, correcting and training in righteousness, so that the man of God may be thoroughly equipped for every good work. (2 Tim. 3:15–17)

Likewise, Psalm 119 details the benefits that God's Word has for our everyday life. I remember the treasure of this passage by applying the acronym B-I-B-L-E to it. God's Word:

- Brightens my path: "Your word is a lamp to my feet and a light for my path" (Ps. 119:105).
- Inspires my life: "Oh, how I love your law! I meditate on it all day long" (Ps. 119:97).
- Builds me up: "Trouble and distress have come upon me, but your commands are my delight" (Ps. 119:143).
- Liberates me: "Direct my footsteps according to your Word; let no sin rule over me" (Ps. 119:133).
- Equips me for living: "How can a young man keep his way pure? By living according to your yord" (Ps. 119:9).

Proverbs 2:4 challenges us to seek for God's wisdom as those who search for hidden treasure. A wonderful example of this treasure is found in the story of Jacob Deshazer. During World War II, Deshazer was one of Doolittle's Raiders who dropped the first bombs on Tokyo. After parachuting into Japan when his plane was shot down, Jacob spent three and a half years in a Japanese prison camp. Barely escaping death by execution, he was given a Bible and by reading it, came to know Christ as his personal Savior.

Following his release and hero's return to America, Jacob answered God's call to go back to Japan to share his testimony. He was instrumental in leading Mitsuo Fuchida to Christ, the captain who led the Japanese bombing raid on Pearl Harbor.[2]

Jacob Deshazer discovered the priceless jewels of truth and salvation in God's Word. So rich was its message that he was compelled to share the treasure even with those who had been his enemies.

THE LIFE EXPERIENCE TREASURE

Through his ability to respond to life's circumstances with wisdom and persistence, George Washington Carver went from an ex-slave orphan to a man who gained fame and notoriety. This outstanding scientist and educator built his legacy by taking ordinary things like a peanut, and discovering intrinsic value in them. Dr. Carver's discoveries from sweet potatoes, soybeans, clay, and peanuts greatly impacted the economy of the American south. They still impact our lives today.[3]

Like Mr. Carver, we can face the adventure of each day with persistence and confidence, anticipating the discovery of the treasures that God has hidden for us and in us. We can do this despite our circumstances. The only thing needed is to become seekers—actively searching out the jewels of wisdom and wonder that God has for us.

God did not create a lump of coal when He spoke the cosmos

into existence. He dazzled the great nothing with everything we see and everything we are. The adventure into which we are invited is to spend our lives searching these treasures out. And unlike the millions hidden in the seas where I live, God's treasures can be found by those who earnestly seek them. Live each day with the anticipation of discovering hidden treasure God has waiting for you, and see how it will bring confidence to that day.

Ask and it will be given to you;
seek and you will find;
knock and the door
will be opened to you.

—MATTHEW 7:7

CHAPTER TWENTY-EIGHT

Confidence in Heaven

WHILE DONNA AND I WERE AT GEORGETOWN COLLEGE, we met a sweet lady in the local church that everybody affectionately referred to as "Granny." She always sat in the same seat down front, raising her frail hand when she received a blessing. After every message I shared, she would approach me and say, "Oh honey, that was just the best sermon ever." I could have preached an absolute flop, but that didn't matter to Granny.

Donna and I were privileged to be in the room with Granny when she took her last breath. I remember sitting down on the side of the bed, watching her as she came in and out of consciousness. When she was alert, we would sing songs about heaven and read the Scripture together.

Then, suddenly, she became very aware and whispered, "Honey, honey, do you see them? Oh, they are so beautiful, and they are coming for me! Oh honey . . ." It was as if God had opened heaven and given her a glimpse into eternity just before she joined Him there. Standing silently in that room, any doubts I had of heaven were washed away with Granny's words. Oh, how the heavens must have rejoiced that day.

As children we don't often think about dying. It isn't till later in life that we understand what all the older folks are smiling about when the choir sings about heaven. The apostle Paul does a good job of directing our attention toward heaven as he writes in Colossians 3:1, "Since, then, you have been raised with Christ, set your hearts on things above, where Christ is seated at the right hand of God."

"*Set* your hearts . . ." In the Greek, this verb is in the present tense, which indicates Paul meant that we should be constantly seeking after the things of heaven. When we keep such a heavenly perspective, life's circumstances begin to take on a fresh outlook.

To many people, heaven is a place of fairy tales—more fiction than fact. But when we begin to recognize the reality of heaven, we uncover a great source of confidence during our days on earth.

Jesus said, "In my Father's house are many rooms; if it were not so, I would have told you. I am going there to prepare a place for you" (John 14:2). With these words, Jesus instilled confidence in His disciples to face the challenges and disappointment of His absence. He gave them—and us—something amazing to look forward to.

A Glimpse of Eternity

In the book of Revelation, we're told that the Spirit of God took John up to heaven to see Jesus being worshipped by the angels and all the saints before him (Rev. 1:1–3). John knew Jesus on earth, watched Him die, saw His empty tomb, and watched Him ascend into heaven. By giving him a glimpse of heaven, God enabled John to affirm those who would place their faith in Jesus Christ. With astonishing confidence, John could assert that heaven—the reward of our faith—is real. It isn't merely a state of mind or a hopeful concept to help us get through today.

I have compiled a "Top Ten" of tangible benefits we will one day enjoy in heaven:

BENEFIT #10: A NEW BODY

Some of us are getting old, and our bodies are deteriorating. I shattered my knees from playing so much football, and now I struggle to walk, let alone run. But I will be running sprints in heaven. When we enter heaven, we will experience vitality unlike anything we've ever known—better than our healthiest, fittest time on earth. Perhaps the greatest benefit of our new bodies is that they will never grow weary or age. Strength and health will be ours forever (1 Cor. 15:53).

BENEFIT # 9: FREEDOM FROM PAIN AND SORROW

When we arrive at our heavenly home, our Father is going to take us in His arms and personally wipe away the hurt from our pasts, our failures, our disappointments, and the crippling pains we've carried in this life. Affirming this fact, John writes:

> And I heard a loud voice from the throne saying, "Now the dwelling of God is with men, and he will live with them. They will be his people, and God himself will be with them and be their God. He will wipe every tear from their eyes. There will be no more death or mourning or crying or pain, for the old order of things has passed away." (Rev. 21:3–4)

In heaven we will finally know perfect peace and joy beyond measure. Our sadness will be forgotten forever.

BENEFIT #8: THE ULTIMATE PERSONAL ESTATE

The Master Carpenter is building you a custom home (John 14:2–3). Obviously no one really knows what this setup will look like, but I like to think some will have country villas, some will have mountain cabins, and others will live on glorious golden seas. What we know for sure is that if we delight ourselves in the Lord, He will give us the desires of our hearts (Ps. 37:4). God knows and loves us here on earth; I think that will translate into unimaginable, spectacular living conditions in heaven.

BENEFIT #7: ALL OUR QUESTIONS ANSWERED

When we get to heaven, we will finally get answers to the questions we've asked on earth. First Corinthians 13:12 says, "Now we see but a poor reflection as in a mirror; then we shall see face to face. Now I know in part; then I shall know fully, even as I am fully known." Imagine finally getting answers to the questions that have simmered in our minds, such as: How long was an actual day when God created the earth? Where did Cain get his wife? Where in the world did God hide the Ark of the Covenant all those years? Some of us will want to ask God why He allowed certain circumstances to occur in our lives. These questions, and all others, will finally have their answers in heaven.

BENEFIT #6: THE GREATEST OF ALL ADVENTURES

Heaven is going to include unending discovery, exploration, and adventure. The Bible talks about a new heaven and earth in Romans 8:18–21:

I consider that our present sufferings are not worth comparing with the glory that will be revealed in us. The creation waits in eager expectation for the sons of God to be revealed. For the creation was subjected to frustration, not by its own choice, but by the will of the one who subjected it, in hope that the creation itself will be liberated from its bondage to decay and brought into the glorious freedom of the children of God.

The Word of God teaches us that this new heaven and earth will be a paradise beyond our imaginations. I believe we will be able to explore this new world, discovering unimaginable beauty always.

BENEFIT #5: HANG OUT WITH HEROES

There are so many biblical characters I have questions for; I can't wait to have conversations with men like Abraham, Isaac, Jacob, Samuel, and Joseph. In Judges 10:1 the Bible mentions a guy named Tola, who "rose up to save Israel." I want to know what he did to be such a hero of the faith. In heaven, I will get the rest of the story. Having full access to the great men and women of God in heaven is a marvelous thing to look forward to. Imagine the conversations we will have over dinner feasts.

BENEFIT #4: FAMILY REUNION

My father came to Christ very late in life. He had always been a good man—hard working and faithful—but he never deliberately lived for God. It wasn't until he went into the hospital to have surgery to remove a cancerous mass that my dad called my son Todd and asked him to visit. God used my father's fear and uncertainty to provide an opportunity for my son to explain to his grandfather his need for Jesus. Todd told me later that tears came to my father's eyes as he bowed his head and prayed to receive Jesus into his heart. A few days after the surgery, my dad caught pneumonia and died.

Praise God, I know my father is in heaven. I can't wait to have him show me around the Holy City. I know that we all have people we can't wait to see. What a reunion it will be!

BENEFIT #3: A CROWN OF LIFE

Paul said, "I press on toward the goal to win the prize for which God has called me heavenward in Christ Jesus" (Phil. 3:14). I, too, am pressing toward that mark when I will receive the crown of life.

In heaven, all of the faithful will be rewarded for their service and faithfulness to God. When the day comes for you to take your last breath, the only thing that will matter is whether your name is written in the Book of Life. God will give you a new name, and He will take the crown of life and place it on your head. Then you will hear those wonderful words, "Well done, good and faithful servant" (Matt. 25:21).

BENEFIT #2: A HEAVENLY TREASURE CHEST

Remember what Jesus said, "Do not store up for yourselves treasures on earth . . . but store up for yourselves treasures in heaven" (Matt. 6:19–20). We lay up treasures in heaven as we invest our lives in the things of God. Each of us will be rewarded according to our acts of service for our King. Every time we love and give to others, we are touching lives with the message of Jesus Christ. We'll discover that the people we took time to care for, talk with, and smile at while on earth are some of our greatest treasures in heaven. Never minimize the impact of your daily actions because they add up to your treasures in heaven.

BENEFIT #1: SEEING JESUS FACE-TO-FACE

"Dear friends, now we are children of God, and what we will be has not yet been made known. But we know that when he appears, we shall be like him, for we shall see him as he is" (1 John 3:2). One day we will see Jesus and we will forget about the troubles of life. His glory will be unlike anything we have ever seen. If we could see only a glimpse of it today, we'd begin living every day with confidence and great anticipation of the full view of our Savior glorified.

The reality is that today finds us a step closer to death, but death is not the end of the road for us. It is the beginning of our every fulfillment and our completion in Christ. Daily we can be confident that we are drawing nearer to ultimate fulfillment and completion—this is a heavenly perspective. With Christ in our hearts, we can face the uncertainty of tomorrow with confidence because we know that God is in control and He has prepared eternity for us.

In this way, love is made complete
among us so that we will have confidence
on the day of judgment, because
in this world we are like him.

—1 JOHN 4:17

CHAPTER TWENTY-NINE

Legacy in the Bones

As the children of Israel trekked across the Sinai Desert, they carried some unusual baggage with them. The priests carried the Tabernacle artifacts along with the Ark of the Covenant. The caravan also included Joseph's coffin. We read in Genesis 50 that Joseph requested his bones be carried back to his homeland and buried there. So four hundred years later when the Israelites set off for the Promised Land, they took Joseph's coffin with them. The sight of the coffin served as a reminder of Joseph's legacy and the continuation of the Israelites' heritage into the future.

God used Joseph to bring His people out of Israel during a famine to take safe haven in Egypt. Now his bones spoke of the need for God's people to be at rest as they prepared to enter the Promised Land. I believe the bones of Joseph were also intended to serve as a symbolic legacy for us today.

Joseph's bones are a constant reminder of God's faithfulness in the lives of His people. Appreciating the importance of this legacy can increase our level of confidence and inspire us to pass this same legacy along to others. Consider with me how a confident legacy is formed, how it is developed, and the way in which we can ensure it continues.

FORMING A LEGACY

Joseph's legacy was formed at his father Jacob's knee. Jacob would have related to his young son how God spared him from the revenge of his brother, Esau, and how God finally reconciled him to his brother (Gen. 33). Jacob would also have shared how God gave him the vision of the angels ascending and descending the ladder into heaven as well as the way he wrestled with the Angel of the Lord until He blessed him (Gen. 32). Jacob would have conveyed to Joseph the truth and greatness of God and the behavior God expected of His people.

The kind of influence we receive is important; it is either helpful in forming God-honoring behavior, or it discourages right thinking and living. Consider, for example, a comparison of two well-known men who lived in America during the 1700s: Max Jukes and Jonathan Edwards.

A professing atheist, Jukes lived a godless life and married a woman who was also an atheist. Among their descendants are numbered 310 paupers, 150 criminals, seven murderers, one hundred drunkards, and more than half of the women were prostitutes. In total, more than five hundred known descendants of Jukes cost the state 1.25 million dollars—today that figure would be much higher.[1]

Compare Jukes with the great American man of God, Jonathan Edwards. He lived at the same time with the same influences, but he married a godly woman. Of the 1,394 known descendants of Jonathan Edwards, thirteen became college presidents, sixty-five were college professors, and three were United States senators. There were thirty judges, a hundred lawyers, sixty physicians, seventy-five army and navy officers, a hundred preachers and missionaries, sixty authors of prominence, one vice-president of the United States, and eighty public officials in other capacities. There were also 295 college graduates, among them governors of states and ministers to foreign countries. In stark contrast, Edwards' descendants didn't cost the state a single penny.[2]

What was true in the past is still true today. The primary way a legacy is formed is through parents' efforts to form their children's character. We know there are many other influences that can impact a child's choices, but I believe that the parents' influence is the most prominent. Certainly, Jukes and Edwards must have had different philosophies when it came to raising their children.

Christian parents need to be proactive in their children's spiritual formation. A combination of family prayer and devotions, regular involvement in ministry, and the daily application of truth by example will greatly impact a child's life. Ultimately, legacy is formed through the commitment of parents who have the vision and loving determination to lead by example.

DEVELOPING A LEGACY

In his book *Extreme Devotion*, Tom White tells of a visitor to Iran who secretly attended an underground church service in the southern part of the country. He had just been released from police custody, and the bruises on his body revealed the treatment he had received. Although he was aware that the police were watching him closely, he continued ministering as much as he could when he wasn't under arrest. He spoke with passion and urged the gathered believers to grow more like Christ, regardless of the cost.

After the service, a foreign guest asked the speaker, "How can you keep such a spirit of hope and cheerfulness in the midst of these troubles?" The Iranian believer answered, "These trials are just tools in God's hands. The tools are designed to make me more holy."[3]

The legacy of a confident Christian life is not developed in powder-puff ease and comfort; it must cost us something. God uses trials as tools to make us more holy—to develop spiritual strength as a part of the legacy we will eventually pass on to others.

LASTING LEGACY

Joseph's legacy impacted the Israelites in the same way it impacts us today. The bones themselves served as a reminder to continue his legacy. The very power of God's work through Joseph's remarkable life is an example to be remembered, celebrated, and carried on until Christ's return.

As I reflect on my life, I can't thank God enough for the legacy that has been passed down to me. Now, the thing that occupies my thinking most is this: When I am gone, the résumé of my accomplishments will mean nothing. What will matter will be my investment into the lives of the young men and women of the generations after me. I want my grandson to walk in confidence that he can draw from a legacy that honors God—that my bones will somehow bring life to him. I know that this will only happen as I live in confidence that the circumstances of my life will build and shape me to be more like Christ. I am confident that the closer I am to Christ, the richer my legacy will become—all to His glory. Live each day knowing you are forming your legacy.

Blessed is the man who fears the LORD,
who finds great delight in his commands.
His children will be mighty in the land;
the generation of the upright will be blessed.

—PSALM 112:1–2

CHAPTER THIRTY

The Reward of Confidence

My first experience visiting someone who was dying in a hospital is one I will never forget. As I sat with the man in that Lexington, Kentucky, hospital and talked about his life, he looked at me sadly and said, "I have lived my entire life in vain. I have wasted my life." What can you say to something like that?

In contrast, I had the complete opposite experience visiting my grandmother when she was near the end of her life. She was a wonderful woman of God, and she had tremendous faith. She didn't recognize me when I entered the room, but when we went to a little chapel where we sat with her and sang old hymns, her memory was jogged; she knew every single hymn. I then asked her to pray with me, and as she prayed, she recognized me and prayed for me by name.

After our time of prayer I said, "Grandma, I love you. Are you okay?" She said that everything was okay and that she was just fine. I saw a sweet smile of confidence on her face as she faced her eternal destiny. It gave me great peace and comfort. This was so different from my experience with the man in Lexington.

There is great reward when we invest our lives and faith in the Lord Jesus Christ. At the end of our lives, we do not have to have regret; we can be infused with the hope of what God has in store for us.

The great apostle Paul made a remarkable statement in writing to his understudy, Timothy. As he drew close to the end of his life while in prison, Paul wrote, "I have fought the good fight, I have finished the race, I have kept the faith. Now there is in store for me the crown of righteousness . . . not only to me, but also to all who have longed for his appearing" (2 Tim. 4:7–8). Paul had a sense of satisfaction that his life stood for something significant and eternal. He had invested his life in the struggle for good, and he knew that he had done his best.

Dr. Bill Bright had tremendous impact for Christ throughout the world. His life was one of vision and submission to Christ. Near the end of his life, my friend John Maxwell and I visited him in Orlando, Florida. As we sat next to him in his room, we could see a distinct glow on Dr. Bright's face even though he struggled for every breath. Of those final days, someone close to him said, "He not only taught us how to live; he also taught us how to die."

Dr. Bright's confidence in his faith caused him to radiate contentment in those final hours. He had fought the good fight, and he challenged John and me to keep fighting that same good fight. He urged us to continue carrying on the mission to see the gospel carried around the world.

I don't know a greater reward of confidence than knowing when you come to the end of your life you have given it your all. When considering this, I often think of the words of Vince Lombardi who asserted, "I firmly believe that any man's finest hour, the greatest fulfillment of all that he holds dear, is the moment when he has worked his heart out in a good cause and lies exhausted on the field of battle—victorious."[1]

This is the fulfillment that Paul found. God charted an extremely difficult course for Paul, and yet he remained focused throughout his life. When he wrote to Timothy, he knew he was very near to the finish line; he also knew that he had charted a clear course for others like Timothy to follow. Even today, his good race profoundly impacts the lives of others, arguably more than any Christian in history.

Someday, we, too, will come to the finish line. In truth, it could be sooner than we think. Regardless of how much more race we have to run, I am convinced that eternity is a reality for all of us. With Christ, we can face eternity with great confidence. In the meantime, between now and that finish line, let's fight well; let's finish the race God has set before us. What remains after that is an inheritance unlike anything we have ever known. Fight with confidence my friends, and fight until the end. Let your confidence be a defining factor of your faith.

Your confidence in Christ will always produce the winning edge in life. Just as Paul, you, too, will be able to boldly declare, "I can do all things through Christ who strengthens me" (Phil. 4:13 NKJV).

And now, dear children, continue in him,
so that when he appears we may
be confident and unashamed
before him at his coming.

—1 JOHN 2:28

Notes

CHAPTER ONE: LIVING IN THE ZONE

1. http://www.quoteland.com/author.asp?AUTHOR_ID=1373.

CHAPTER TWO: YOUR JOURNEY MATTERS

1. From the PBS presentation transcript, "The American Experience: The Donner Party," 1997, http://www.pbs.org/wgbh/amex/donner/filmmore/pt.html; http://en.wikipedia.org/wiki/Donner_party.
2. Ibid.
3. Lee Strobel, *The Case for Christ* (Grand Rapids: Zondervan, 1998).

CHAPTER FOUR: THE CONFIDENCE OF A CHAMPION

1. Michael Johnson, "Wariner Must Have Faith in His Approach," August 8, 2004, http://www.telegraph.co.uk/sport/main.jhtml?xml=/sport/2004/08/23/sojohn23.xml.
2. Bob Baum, College Sports TV, August 13, 2004, http://www.cstv.com/sports/c-track/stories/081304aah.html.

CHAPTER FIVE: HANG WITH CHAMPIONS

1. Paul Newberry, College Sports TV, August 19, 2004, http://www.cstv.com/sports/c-swim/stories/082004aal.html.

2. Darrell Hamlett, "Wilkinson, Soldati share passion for diving, God," *Conroe Courier*, July 17, 2004.

CHAPTER SIX: GET TOUGH

1. Penny Lent, "Mission of Love: Son befriends father's murderer on the mission field," El Cajon: *Christian Times*, Northwest Edition, March 2001.
2. http://en.wikipedia.org/wiki/Fanny_Crosby.

CHAPTER SEVEN: MISTAKEN IDENTITY

1. Rev. J. Wilbur Chapman, D.D., *The Life and Work of Dwight Lyman Moody (1837–1899)*, (London: James Nisbet and Company, 1900).
2. http://www.grahamfestival.org/franklin.html.
3. Erwin McManus, *An Unstoppable Force: Daring to Become the Church God Had in Mind* (Loveland, CO: Group Publishing, 2001), 201.
4. Dwight Lyman Moody and James S. Bell, Sr., *The D. L. Moody Collection: The Highlights of His Writings, Sermons, Antidotes, and Life Story* (Chicago: Moody Press, 1998), 102.

CHAPTER EIGHT: FEAR TO FAITH

1. Norma McCorvey with Gary Thomas, *Won by Love* (Nashville: Thomas Nelson, 1998).
2. David Wilkerson, *The Cross and the Switchblade* (New York: Jove Books, 1962).

CHAPTER NINE: RECOVERING OUR FUMBLES

1. Story adapted from Web site, http://www.omegafaith.org/mulesense.htm.

2. Rick Weinberg, http://sports.espn.go.com/espn/espn25/ story?page=moments/94.

3. http://www.outercourt.com/basic/source/pearl6/quotes.txt.

4. John Maxwell, *Failing Forward: Turning Mistakes into Stepping Stones for Success,* (Nashville: Thomas Nelson, 2000).

5. http://www.baseball-reference.com/a/aaronha01.shtml.

6. http://www.baseball-reference.com/r/ruthba01.shtml.

CHAPTER ELEVEN: CONFIDENCE IN GOD'S COVENANTS

1. Richard Foster, *Streams of Living Water: Celebrating the Great Traditions of Christian Faith* (HarperSanFrancisco, 2001), 210.

2. "The Life of the Altar and the Tent," http://www.ministrybooks.org/watchman-nee-books.cfm, 86. Life of the Altar and the Tent, The.

CHAPTER THIRTEEN: CONFIDENCE WITH COMMUNICATION

1. Kevin Miller, http://www.preachingtoday.com/23450.

2. http://www.britainexpress.com/History/bio/dickens.htm.

3. http://www.new-life.net/lying.htm.

4. William J. Bennett, *The Index of Leading Cultural Indicators: Facts and Figures on the State of American Society* (New York: Simon and Schuster, 1994), 102–103.

5. Bill Hybels, "Your Wife: Fit to be Treasured," *New Man,* Jan/Feb 1995, 17–21.

CHAPTER EIGHTEEN: WHEN BAD THINGS HAPPEN

1. Jim Collins, *Good to Great* (New York: Harper Collins, 2001), 85.

CHAPTER TWENTY: INVESTING FOR ETERNITY

1. Mrs. Howard Taylor, *Borden of Yale '09* (Philadelphia: China Inland Mission, 1926).
2. http:/www.joyfulministry.com/walkf.htm.
3. Bryan Chapell, *Each for the Other* (Grand Rapids: Baker, 2006), 14–15.
4. Jack Kelley, *USA Today* reporter, from his message, "The Stories Behind the Headlines," given at Evangelical Press Association convention in May 2000.

CHAPTER TWENTY-TWO: THE PLAYBOOK FOR CONFIDENT LIVING

1. Lew Wallace, *Lew Wallace: An Autobiography*, (New York: Harper & Brothers Publishing, 1906).
2. Peter Deison, *The Priority of Knowing God: Taking Time with God When There Is No Time*, (Grand Rapids: Discovery House Publishers, 1990), 80–81.

CHAPTER TWENTY-THREE: TRAIN FOR VICTORY

1. Corrie ten Boom, *Tramp for the Lord* (New York: Jove Books, 1974), 61.
2. *God's Little Devotional Book for Leaders* (Colorado Springs, CO: Honor Books, 2001), 230.

CHAPTER TWENTY-FOUR: THE DANGERS OF COMPROMISE

1. *Daily Manna*, (Chicago: Moody Press, 1981), September 10.
2. Chuck Colson, *Born Again* (Grand Rapids: Chosen Books, 2004).

CHAPTER TWENTY-FIVE: WE ALL NEED A GPS

1. http://en.wikipedia.org/wiki/Korean_Air_Flight_007.

2. Michael Richardson, *Amazing Grace: The Authorized Biography of Dr. Bill Bright, Founder of Campus Crusade for Christ* (Colorado Springs, CO: WaterBrook Press, 2001), 91–96.

3. Bob Mumford, *Take Another Look at Guidance* (Cookeville, TN: Lifechangers Publishers, 1993), 87.

CHAPTER TWENTY-SIX: DRIVEN BY A DREAM

1. Story adapted from http://www.icgn.us/cutethings.html.

2. Rev. J. Wilbur Chapman D.D., *The Life and Work of Dwight Lyman Moody (1837–1899),* Ibid.

3. Nell Mohney, "Beliefs Can Influence Attitudes," *Kingsport Times*, July 25, 1986, 4B.

4. http://www.crhra.org/pdfs/September2004.pdf#search=%22%22conquered%20the%20temptation%22%20peter%20lowe%22.

5. *Earl Nightingale's The Strangest Secret Millennium 2000 Gold Record Recording*, audio CD (Keys Company, Inc., 1999).

6. Matthew Scully, *Viktor Frankl at Ninety: An Interview* (First Things 52, April 1995), 39–43.

7. Gary Karmer, ed., *George Washington Carver: In His Own Words* (Columbia: The University of Missouri Press, 1987), 1.

8. As cited in a speech by Graham P. Spanier, President of Penn State University, http://president.psu.edu/speeches/articles/123.html.

9. http://www.pbs.org/lostliners.titanic.html.

10. Paul Simon, *Freedom's Champion Elijah Lovejoy* (Carbondale: Southern Illinois University Press, 1994).

CHAPTER TWENTY-SEVEN: HIDDEN TREASURE

1. Hellen Keller, *The Story of My Life* (New York: Bantam Classics, 1990).

2. Jacob Deshazer, *I Was a Prisoner of Japan* (Columbus: Bible Meditation League, 1950).

3. Gary Kramer, ed. *George Washington Carver,* Ibid.

CHAPTER TWENTY-NINE: LEGACY IN THE BONES

1. http://www.ravenhill.org/edwards.htm.

2. Ibid.

3. Tom White, *Extreme Devotion* (Nashville, TN: W Publishing Group, 2001), 165.

CHAPTER THIRTY: THE REWARD OF CONFIDENCE

1. http://www.vincelombardi.com/about/quotes/winning.html.